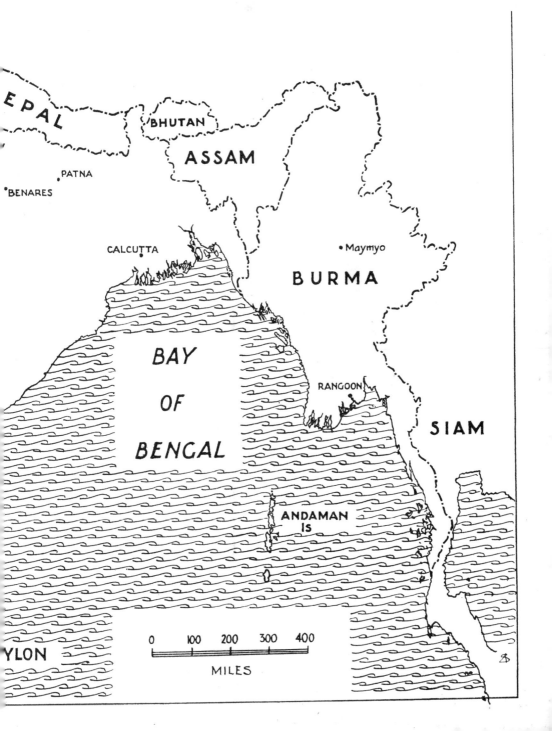

TIBET

EPAL

BHUTAN

ASSAM

•PATNA

•BENARES

CALCUTTA
•

•Maymyo

BURMA

BAY

OF

BENGAL

RANGOON

SIAM

ANDAMAN
IS

YLON

0   100   200   300   400

MILES

The Viceroy's Wife

By the same author

RULE OF THREE

The Viceroy's Wife

Letters of Alice, Countess of Reading,
from India, 1921–25

by

IRIS BUTLER

HODDER AND STOUGHTON

Printed in Great Britain for Hodder and Stoughton Limited, St. Paul's
House, Warwick Lane, London, E.C.4. by Ebenezer Baylis and Son,
Ltd., The Trinity Press, Worcester, and London

TO EVA

Acknowledgements

These letters were written by Lady Reading to her son, Gerald, 2nd Marquess of Reading, and his wife Eva, to be circulated in the family. There are six boxes of them, all in Alice Reading's own hand. Only one box is entirely personal in which each letter starts, "Dearest Children . . ." All the other letters start, "Dearest People . . ." I am grateful to Eva, Marchioness of Reading, for putting these letters in my hands and for the suggestion made by her and her daughter, Lady Joan Zuckerman, that I should write a book round them. Lady Joan has also taken great trouble to check my typescript and give me much valuable help. I am grateful to the Trustees of the Reading papers, the 3rd Marquess of Reading, the Dowager Marchioness of Reading (Baroness Swanborough), and Sir Solly Zuckerman for permission to use the letters and print them.

Miss Yvonne FitzRoy has kindly allowed me to use her Diary, which has illuminated every step of my way.

The late Mr. Victor Butler gave me permission to use the letters, now in the India Office Library, of his father Sir Harcourt Butler, for which I am most grateful.

I am grateful to Mr. Martin Gilbert for permission to use footnotes from his book, *Servant of India* (Longmans, 1966).

Grateful thanks to the Librarian and staff of the India Office Library and the London Library for much help over footnotes and illustrations.

I am grateful to Mr. Hallam Ashley, F.R.P.S. for the care and skill he has given to reproducing illustrations.

Also to Miss Fatehma Abdul Ghani and Miss Maureen Travis, Librarian, India House.

I am grateful to Sir Arthur Willert for information about Lady Reading's time in Washington as Ambassadress.

I am grateful to Mrs. G. R. D. Baines for permission to read her late husband's notes on his time as A.D.C. to Lord Reading. I am most grateful, as always, to Mrs. Robert Atterton for preparing and tidying up my typescript for publication, and making the index.

Finally I am much in the debt of my brother, Lord Butler of Saffron Walden, for checking my work for political indiscretions.

Contents

Illustrations

KEY TO ACKNOWLEDGEMENTS

1 The Lady Joan Zuckerman
2 The Marquess of Reading
3 Miss Yvonne FitzRoy
4 The India Office Library
5 Author
6 Eva, Marchioness of Reading

Introduction

Mr. E. M. Forster, in his life of G. Lowes Dickinson, quotes the latter as saying: "And why can't the races meet? Simply because the Indians *bore* the English." Pandit Nehru quotes this statement in his *Autobiography* (The Bodley Head, 1936, p. 28) and follows it up by saying: "The Englishman and the Indian are always posing to each other and naturally they feel uncomfortable in each other's company. Each bores the other and is glad to get away from him to breathe freely and move naturally again." These opinions must be examined honestly by those of us who imagined, when we lived in India, that we were a success. Boredom is a dangerous sensation; a stronger word should be found for that which can kill affection, create distrust and destroy the nerves as completely as sorrow or cruelty. If it was true that we bored each other, the two races, then no wonder so many bitter words have been poured out about our association since it came to an end.

My personal experience does not lead me to endorse these accusations of mutual boredom. I can never remember a time when the thought of India (the whole peninsula) did not immediately evoke emotion and stimulate interest. In fact, memories of India and my Indian friends have lightened hours of acute boredom since I left them all. I know I was blessed in coming of a family which (on my mother's side) served India for three generations. I also owed much to my father who insisted that I should learn at least one main language (Urdu) well enough to conduct a reasonable conversation, though I was too lazy to master the script and have regretted it ever since. Many Englishwomen suffered boredom and homesickness because home-making, motherhood, security and the comfort of family life were all precarious and constantly disrupted. Men were seldom bored for they had interesting work to do, marvellous sport and opportunities for an especially masculine type of life such as suits Englishmen. The "Lady Sahibs" at the top of the pyramid missed their ancestral voices, they often felt that society in India was not equal to their needs. But since, in those days,

13

no ancestral voice spoke louder than that which called for *noblesse oblige*, these ladies all did their duty nobly.

I find it interesting that G. Lowes Dickinson and Pandit Nehru used the word "English" rather than "British". It always seemed to me that those Europeans happiest in India and most successful in their relationships with Indians were not pure English. Celtic, Latin or Jewish blood is often the secret of sympathy with the East. Lady Reading's ancestral voices were very ancient and subtly different from most of her predecessors. Her mind was untrained, but it was a very active and perceptive one and she came from a background which did not despise such a gift. She was also able to keep in step with the quick emotional reactions of Eastern people, and to respond to them without prejudice. I knew her quite well; she was kind and friendly to girls, of whom I was one, in the official world of Delhi and Simla in the nineteen-twenties. In those days young married women had the best of social life. Most of the girls came straight from school without any grooming for an adult world. Our lack of sophistication would make a modern schoolgirl gasp. I went to all official functions with my parents and found the Members of Council and Generals who took one in to dinner easier to cope with than the glorious young men who led one up to talk to Her Ex. afterwards. The "Aides" appeared to me like gods walking. One of these dazzling creatures took a brief fancy to me and my mother must have thought well of him as he was allowed to take me dancing after dinner one night at Maidens Hotel in Delhi. On no account was I ever allowed to dine alone with a man; apparently dancing was thought safer. I wore my best frock, an affair of floating chiffon panels each with a little weight on the end. All my partner said to me that evening was: "This is a bloody awful dress you are wearing, something keeps clashing against my shins." We had not got into short skirts by that time (1923). Lady Reading remarks on Princess Arthur of Connaught's short skirts two years later.

I was born in Simla and spent the first four summers of my life there. So to return at the age of seventeen seemed like going home. I recognised paths along which I walked with Nanny and my brother in the past, the rickshaw trailing behind and always (so it seemed) a dog barking in the far distance. Nanny told us that all dogs were mad and that the huge cobra-headed "Lords and Ladies" growing on the roadside in the rains were deadly poison. No-one ever suggested poison to us in any other way. Nanny loved India as much as we did and ran the household in partnership with Ghokal, my father's bearer who served

him for all the years he stayed in India; they grew from young man-
hood to middle-age together. Neither Ghokal nor Nanny did very
much hard work but they were an impressive team. We were always
told never to disturb Ghokal between the hours of 2 and 5 p.m. as he
was a very high-caste man and had to perform a number of ceremonies
connected with his main meal of the day. He never came near the
dining room because our food was unclean to him, but he did make tea
in the early morning for my parents which he carried as far as the
bedroom door, but no further, since to enter would have been im-
proper. Even when my father was a Governor, he always got out of bed
to fetch the tea-tray from outside his bedroom door. He wrote a Collect
about it, praying for strength to "feel after and find Tea". The caste
system in private households became much more lax as years went by
because my generation could not afford as many servants as our parents
employed, but in Viceregal circles the one-man-one-job system maintained a firm hold. It irritated Lady Reading when she first met it
though she settled down to it as we all did in the end, realising how it
helped poor people in a land of high unemployment and gave that sense
of continuity (son succeeding father) and tribal cohesion which is now
called paternalistic and undemocratic. In addition to Ghokal there were
many other servants who came and went and I remember with especial
affection the syces who led my pony in Simla and also Mother's big
Australian horse, By Chance, on whom I was allowed to ride out to tea
sometimes, perched high on a side-saddle in my best bib and tucker,
much more fun than a rickshaw. I remember waking from a deep sleep
one night to be carried into the verandah by my father to see Halley's
Comet streak across the Himalaya. This episode photographed the
great mountains on my mind for ever.

My childhood winters were spent in Rajasth'an and Lahore, so
Delhi became a new place to discover when I came out from school. I
went for long, long rides alone into the great plain where the Durbar of
1911 took place, returning home at dusk with the mist rising as high as
the pony's withers, and the shanty dwellings at the edge of the cultivated land pricked out by points of light—cooking fires on the ground
round the huts. It never occurred to me that I was an alien, that I had
no right to be there, that I was a member of a master race. There was
no talk of fear, though my father had but recently come from the
Punjaub and all the troubles following the Rowlatt Bills. My parents
never prevented me from riding out alone.

We had many Indian friends, notably the Shafis, who appear in
Lady Reading's letters. And there were splendid figures from the
Punjaub. Sir Umer Hyat Khan, head of the Tiwana Clan, came south
for meetings of the Council of State, bringing with him his hawks, his
hounds and what my mother called his "Dhuniwassails" (Liegemen–
Gaelic). He gave delightful hawking parties in the early dawn on the
Jumna plain, across the Bridge of Boats on the Meerut road. Rising in
the dark we motored out to meet our horses and the wild northern
men, profiles matching the birds on their wrists. They flew a gay
goshawk at hares, and smaller hawks stooped on partridge and quail.
It was a more natural sport than shooting.

One Christmas we went to Bikaner and another to Kotah, a Rajput
State Lady Reading never saw, where my father had served when we
were children. We called the Maharao "Andatta"—Breadgiver—as his
people did. I had not seen him since those nursery days but it all came
back to me, including two romantic figures named Apji Koela and Apji
Pelita, names conjuring up giants and wizards, who turned out to be
jolly gentlemen, friends of my parents. The title "Apji" corresponds
to "Himself" in Ireland and the territorial names used of landowners in
Scotland—Lochiel, Tullibardine.

The princes were either cosmopolitan or traditional. In either case
their hospitality was boundless and sometimes abused, their generosity
towards charitable schemes unlimited, as Lady Reading often records.
They did spread their wealth for the public good and it is not for us to
pry into their motives. They are the victims of history, as we are too,
and all the other protagonists of absolute power who have "abode an
hour or two" in that land of conquest and re-conquest.

Lady Reading and her daughter-in-law, Eva Erleigh, were the first
people to open my mind to anything other than my personal interests.
Lady Erleigh and her mother, the first Lady Melchett, were pioneers in
maternity and child welfare work in Great Britain before these branches
of social service became the sole responsibility of public authorities.
There is no doubt that Lady Reading was influenced by this when she
decided to make maternity and child welfare her chief concern in India.
After I married, I attempted to carry out some of the lessons I had
learnt from working with Eva Erleigh. I had heard a good deal about
Lady Reading's schemes in India which my mother, when she became
a Governor's wife, forwarded in her own sphere of influence. But I was
always a "chhota memsahib" and as such could initiate nothing. Only

"burra memsahibs" could raise money and if one happened to be beneath the sway of a burra memsahib who was not interested in social service, there was nothing one could do about it. The only people free of such frustrations were the Missions and they welcomed any voluntary help as long as it was given efficiently and affectionately, and they asked nothing about one's personal beliefs or worship; there was too much work to be done for suffering people to allow time for proselytising or splitting hairs between denominations. Lady Reading made friends with missionaries and doctors as well as helping them with money and official visits. All the "Lady Sahibs" started up funds and organisations which bore their names.

How was it possible to be bored for a moment with so much to learn and do and see? So much colour and contrast, above all so much response to any advance made in friendship towards Indians? Yet Pandit Nehru spoke truth when he said we were not always at ease with each other. I remember often feeling uncertain about what was expected of me. Sometimes one tried too hard and became unnatural. I once prepared to give an anthology of English poetry to an Indian friend and suddenly realised there was a dreary little poem in it called, "A Private of the Buffs", about an English private who refused to kow-tow to some Chinese who had captured him and so was beheaded. Meanwhile some Indians did as they were told and survived—

> "Let dusky Indians whine and kneel;
> "An English lad must die."

I tore out the page in an agony of embarrassment. It must have surprised her to receive a mutilated gift, and I feel shamed to this day that I did not trust in her affection and wit. It never occurred to me then, nor indeed since, to criticise the dusky Indians of this poem. It was not their quarrel. As the wife of an Indian Army Officer I came to know the Indian soldier well, and his wife and children, of several races and faiths. When I was nursing Indian troops after the retreat from Burma in 1942, they poured in to hospital by the hundred, day after day, literally dying on their feet of exhaustion, dysentry, malaria, pneumonia, starvation. We ran out of drugs, beds, blankets, even water throughout a dreadful two weeks till the rush dwindled. One man said to me: "I have fought for the Sircar (the government) and you cannot give me a bed to die on." I marvelled then, as I often have before and since, at the devotion and loyalty of the Indian Army. Now, when the

2

sons of old soldiers come to England, they frequently meet with discourtesy and misunderstanding. They were good enough to fight and die for us in war after war, the reasons for which were never explained to them.

When my husband went to work for the Nizam of Hyderabad, we came into a society where there were few, if any, inhibitions between the races, and certainly no boredom on our side. I hope none on theirs, but they would be too courteous to say even if it were so. There were enormous contrasts of sophistication and simplicity in this state. It seemed to epitomise one's life in India. On the one hand, a Nawab speaking several European languages would correct me for reading Renan's *Vie de Jésus* because it denies the Incarnation and, as a Christian, I had no right to contemplate such an idea even if he, as a Moslem, did so. On the other hand, there was a purdah lady whom I loved. She was a witch of moderately benign practices, some of which she demonstrated to me when we were alone together chewing *pan* and talking about our neighbours and our children in a womanly sort of way. There was a General in command of the armies in Hyderabad who, when I asked his advice as to how to make a success of my stay in the state, told me: "Keep your mouth shut and your bowels open." The state allotted to us as a dwelling the top floor of a huge old stone house on a hill, looking across a lake. In the garden the two domes of the Observatory stood embowered in trees. The State Astronomer, Mr. Bhaskaran, had his office on the ground floor of our house. He was a learned scientist who corresponded in several languages with astronomers all over the world. He allowed me to have "Astronomy Parties" at which my guests were shown the moon through his telescopes. After that we all repaired to the wide verandah overlooking the lake to have supper and to admire the moon once more in the place we were accustomed to see her, making a path on the water. Mr. Bhaskaran, an orthodox Brahmin, joined us, sitting a little apart for we were untouchables and our food pollution to him. He sipped water with dignity, kind, clever and friendly—but apart. Remembering those days, I feel that our life in India was like looking at the moon through a telescope. We saw everything enlarged, we were far away from what we saw, we only looked and wondered, inexhaustibly interested, emotionally moved, perhaps a little afraid, and then withdrew to the life we knew.

This book is a period piece. It tells of a simple approach to an immensely complicated problem, a personal approach, from the heart. The life it describes seems as distant as a Grecian Urn. Between that life and ours of to-day lies a deep gulf full of dark shapes—war, torture, deceit, destruction, betrayal, suffering of the innocent. The air around us is thick with blame and recrimination. I have found it a refreshment to turn away and listen for a while to voices of good will from the other side of the divide.

CHAPTER I

Once Upon a Time

*"C'est aux hommes à faire des grandes choses,
c'est aux femmes à les inspirer."*

Comte Ségur

THIS is the story of one woman's contact with India and the impact of India upon her. Political issues in India will keep the historians busy for many generations yet; personal issues are mostly buried in sad cemeteries. When the story of the British Indian period can be told without bitterness, the love and friendship which lit up some corners of that strange partnership will be more worthy of remembrance than the mistakes of politicians. Those who write about British India to-day like to stress unhappy personal contacts. The incidents in railway carriages, the arrogance of the club, the hauteur on social occasions—these are set down often from hearsay, or arise from the personal prejudices of the writers and speakers. It is time for some record of kindness and courtesy to be remembered. Some of us fell in love with India and tried to show it. In fact, many of us were quite unconscious of any need for suspicion and rejection on either side. We took our life in India for granted, it was home.

Alice Reading spent only five years in India and those in isolation at the top of the pyramid. She had no tradition of empire in her blood, no family graves to visit, no memories from childhood. She knew nothing whatever about the country when she went there and remained somewhat vague about Indian history and creeds to the end of her stay. She could not understand or speak any Indian language. But she loved India. These personal letters, meant only for the eyes of her family, prove that she responded eagerly to her vivid, luxurious and exciting life and she found that Indians, as they always do, came more than half-way to meet her interest and sympathy.

Her husband was deliberately chosen by a Liberal government to administer a liberal experiment in India. This experiment, known as the Montagu-Chelmsford Reforms, seemed grudging and deficient to leaders of nationalist opinion in India. These were men of intelligence and education well aware of the history of British Indian relations from the eighteenth century onwards. They knew of the far more integrated society of the early days of the East India Company. The time when rulers of the calibre of Warren Hastings and Mountstuart Elphinstone without doubt looked forward to handing over power to Indians themselves. The rulers of India in those days were men of the Age of Reason. Dedicated to a life-long service without remission, they were deeply versed in the languages, culture and customs of the people they ruled; they were latitudinarian in religion, unprejudiced, tolerant. After them came the great figures of the nineteenth century, men of a more rigid caste, possibly of greater integrity but lesser sympathy, fanatical in religion, certain of their superiority. Their links with home were strengthened by the opening of the Suez Canal; English women came out in greater numbers to found completely English homes, Indian women disappeared further behind the purdah,[1] the rift of misunderstanding between the races widened. Macaulay's minute on education, insisting on the teaching of English in all higher grades, introduced Indians to the liberal philosophers of the nineteenth century. Thus at one and the same time doors to freedom of thought were opened while doors to freedom of action were shut.

The war of 1914–18 broke down many doors and Indians were justified in expecting that the immense efforts they had put into helping to win it would be rewarded by a greater measure of political freedom. It was to meet this legitimate expectation that the Liberal government of Lloyd George sent the Secretary of State for India, Edwin Montagu,[2] to evolve with the Viceroy, Lord Chelmsford,[3] a preliminary constitution giving Indians greater political power, and inaugurating an embryonic form of parliamentary democracy. Edwin Montagu believed implicitly in freedom for India; Rufus Isaacs shared that belief. It is significant that these two brilliant men were both Jewish, a race that has maintained freedom for centuries in the face of fearful odds. But they had to steer the frail barque of their beliefs through heavy storms. The retiring Viceroy gave little more than his name to the Reforms; he was described by the most astute of his provincial governors as having "the qualities that adorn private life". Thus Lord Reading took over a confused and divided country, ripe for anti-British demonstrations and communal strife, with the Civil Service embittered and uneasy about the future.

"*Les hommes font les lois, les femmes font les moeurs.*"[4] These letters
are a chronicle of "*moeurs*". A great deal of high-minded and brilliant
political work in India was vitiated by insensitive personal contacts.
The urbane atmosphere of the eighteenth century could not be restored
in the twentieth, but the choice of Lord Reading as Viceroy in 1921
was peculiarly happy in that he and his wife were free of the normal
prejudices of the English ruling caste. She had her own prejudices but
they were not those of creed or colour. She was an old-fashioned
woman, proud to walk behind her husband, to be, as it were, in purdah.
She was a much-honoured wife and mother, extremely secure in the
family, in the Jewish tradition. This, though she did not realise it,
gave her a link with Indians.

An ancient Hindu scripture, *The Laws of Manu*, says: "Where
females are honoured, there the deities are pleased." The power and
position of women in eastern society is often misunderstood. They have
rights of their own as part of Hindu religious philosophy, and in
Islamic law; this gives them confidence and dignity, especially in later
life. Alice Reading was a grandmother when she came to India. She
had a status which would be instantly recognisable to Indians who
often found younger Englishwomen inexplicable and shocking.

She does not write very much about politics. Her letters took three
weeks to get to their destination by which time political news would be
stale and she could not repeat anything confidential. So she threw her
heart and energy into what she felt was her own sphere. Entertaining
Indians and British alike, making personal contacts which might be of
use to the Viceroy and, above all, doing everything she could for the
women and children of India. She is often accused of enjoying her
position. It is strange to use the word "accuse" in this context, but such
comments are always pejorative. Why should she not enjoy rather than
"grizzle" (a favourite word in her letters)? Once her initial homesickness evaporated, her letters glow with enjoyment even when she writes
in pain and illness. Enjoyment of beauty, luxury and drama; enjoyment of scents, flowers and colours; enjoyment of people. Above all,
enjoyment of her power to do some good for the women and children
of India, enjoyment of her husband's success and enjoyment of his
enjoyment. It is reported that when the Irwins took over from the
Readings in Bombay in April, 1926, Lady Irwin remarked on Lady
Reading's "pallor" and this was attributed to chagrin at ceasing to
be "Queen". At that point Alice Reading was at the lowest ebb of her

strength; she had stayed in India after a severe operation in order to
be with her husband up to the end of his term of office. A less courageous woman would have gone home at the New Year, and there is no
doubt that this last effort shortened her life. Of course she minded
saying farewell to India—she had left some of her heart there. Never
was any woman less deluded by "*folie de grandeur*".

She grew up in an old-fashioned Jewish home of great rectitude and
discipline. Her father, Albert Cohen, by nature a recluse and scholar,
had to make his way in a business world from which he retreated at the
end of every day to secluded family life. His children grew up in a
patriarchal atmosphere, kindly but despotic. Alice went to day-school
and learnt to speak French and German fluently and she enjoyed the
musical and artistic advantages of cultivated Jewish society. But it was
not the custom then for a girl to develop a trained mind, nor did she
get any opportunities for country life, sport, travel and the freedoms
enjoyed by the sort of girl from whom a future Vicereine might be
drawn. There was no tradition of government in her family.

At the age of eighteen she met young Rufus Isaacs at a dancing class.
He was then at the beginning of his studies for the Bar, very handsome,
very gay and showing no special signs of future greatness. In fact, his
fortunes were at a low ebb as he had been hammered on the Stock
Exchange for being unable to meet his obligations. He and Alice
Cohen fell in love and decided to marry, in spite of the violent opposition of her family. Like the heroine of a melodrama, she sank into a
decline and thus forced her parents to consent to her engagement.

Rufus Isaacs was always a man of great charm and sweetness though
in later years he became so reserved that it often proved difficult for
ordinary people to penetrate his graceful but adamant façade. Sir
Francis Oppenheimer met them both in the early days of their marriage.
He became a life-long friend and his testimony of them comes straight
from the heart with the vitality and colour that are missing from
comments of the friends and biographers who were not admitted to
their innermost circle. He describes Alice Isaacs as "a striking young
woman, tall and erect with an excellent figure and an impressive gait,
her head crowned by masses of blond hair."[5] He was impressed by the
gaiety and vigour of this young couple and their radiant devotion to
each other. Alice insisted that her husband should continue at the Bar,
regardless of the small income on which they had to live. On their
wedding day the future Lord Chief Justice received what was only his

second brief. By the time their only child was born they were able to take a small furnished house at Brighton for holidays where, as Gerald grew older, both parents spent much time with him and his Nanny Squires, who never left the service of the family, accompanying them even to India in her old age. Writing from thence when homesick, Alice Reading says how comforting she found it to be able to talk over old times with Squires.

It is difficult to trace the history of her poor health because she never discussed it in detail with friends or even her family. A suggestion of "malade imaginaire" has hung about her. Sir Francis Oppenheimer says "she became an invalid before reaching middle age and so dropped out of the social picture in which he became one of the leading figures."[6] But he and other writers on this period often mention dinner parties at Curzon Street (the Readings' town house) and week-ends at Foxhill, their home in the constituency after his entry into politics. She entertained in her own home with particular zest and grace, but she also spent many hours on a sofa or in bed. Anyone reading her letters from India must realise that her maladies were far from imaginary. She was a most courageous woman, and it was not then the fashion to shout medical details from the housetops. She did not have the type of personality which is prepared to enter whole-heartedly into the social hurly-burly that accompanies political life. A brilliant man, no matter how modest his start, will very soon be welcomed in any social circle, up to the highest, if he is successful, amusing and personally attractive. It is much harder for his wife unless she is prepared to work for it by incessant entertaining and relentless attention to being in the right place at the right time from one year's end to another. Alice Isaacs did not have that sort of ambition. She believed in her husband and knew his quality, she encouraged him to set forth on his own and he returned to share with her everything her health had caused her to miss. All her life until she went to India, people had to come to her — she did not go forth to meet them.

Rufus Isaacs entered the House of Commons as Liberal member for Reading in 1904 and went on to be Solicitor General early in 1910 and Attorney General later in that year. In 1913 he became Lord Chief Justice and Baron Reading and, finally, Ambassador to Washington and Earl of Reading in 1918. This appointment must have seemed a great challenge to Alice Reading. It meant leaving England and battling with her ill-health in the midst of official rather than private entertaining though the exigencies of wartime curtailed this necessity. It also made the first break in a custom established by her widowed mother who, since the death of the patriarch, had developed a demanding and possessive nature. She liked to visit her favourite daughter every afternoon, and because Alice was a semi-invalid, she was exceptionally vulnerable, and it is unlikely that Lady Reading would have faced five years in India if her mother had not died in 1920. And Lord Reading would not have taken the Viceroyalty without his wife. When the appointment was offered to him, she managed to get her doctor on her side before her husband could consult him. She was a determined woman and the doctor agreed to tell Lord Reading that his wife's health was equal to the climate and the strenuous life that would await the Viceroy's wife.

The Readings landed in India on April 2nd, 1921, and two days later left for Delhi. They were alight with optimism and it was reported that "Reading seems to have made a good start. They say he is unconventional, that he laughed when told that ladies had to curtsey and waved his hand at Lady Reading when she did it. That he asks all and sundry why India should be a difficult country to govern, whether humanity is different here from elsewhere. A very suitable spirit!"[7] Lord Reading had to curb his idealism to make the system work, since "Politics is the art of the possible" and no Viceroy ever understood that maxim better. This then was the political background against which these extremely personal letters were written.

CHAPTER II

A Plain Tale

"A good land, a land of brooks of water, of fountains and depths that
spring out of valleys and hills; a land of wheat, and barley, and vines,
and fig trees, and pomegranates; a land of oil olive, and honey."

> Deuteronomy, 8. Quoted in *Views Of Simla*
> by Captain G. P. Thomas of the 64th Regiment,
> Bengal Infantry. 1846.

WRITING to her son and daughter-in-law[1] from Delhi on
April 6th, 1921, her first letter from her first official residence, Alice Reading says:

In spite of all the crowd I miss you both terribly. When I came out of the
Convocation Hall (Bombay) when H.E. was sworn in I never felt so
alone in my life! Not a soul I knew to give me a hug and wish me well,
only strange, strange faces everywhere. The penalties of a great position!
No-one has any idea what the position is. Buckingham Palace, Windsor,
everything simple in comparison with the show and glitter (necessary,
I understand, to impress with power). Never two people had so many
well-wishers. God grant the 1,000th part comes true.

The Viceregal party stayed in Delhi only twenty-four hours before
moving on to Dehra Dun in the foothills of the Himalayas, there to
recuperate from the arrival and give the household time to move to
Simla. They were impressed by the Viceregal train which Miss Yvonne
FitzRoy (Lady Reading's secretary)[2] describes in her diary:

We had heard much of the Viceregal train, even the Russian Imperial
train could not compete with it for luxury, we were told, and were not
disappointed. But all the luxury in the world cannot defeat this climate . . .
No screen was the least use against the dust — the fans merely circulated a
hot, exhausted wind — door-handles nearly too hot to touch — beds far
too hot to lie on — clothes, a literally painful necessity — and the hopeful
rush to the cold water tap greeted by a flow of nicely boiled water.

Though only so short a time in Delhi, Alice Reading immediately obeyed
what would seem to have been a law of nature among proconsular ladies.

Altho' only 24 hours here [she writes] have found out so much I candidly disapprove of and must change. I realise a Vicereine's work never ceases however good her Staff is for there are thousands of things a mere man never notices, and before three months are over my head the Viceregal Lodges will be run quite differently.

In due course her interior decorations, her mauves and greys, were obliterated by Lady Irwin,[3] then the mauve returned with Lady Willingdon.[4] Lady Linlithgow[5] then cast forth the stone gnomes and rabbits set up in the Moghul gardens by Lady Willingdon at the great new palace which was only foundation-high in the Readings' day.

She writes from Dehra Dun:

We are neither of us at our best. Passed a terrible day yesterday, ending in a sand storm (*vide* "The Garden of Allah"[6]); everything, hair, clothes, luggage, impregnated with sand; you feel gritty all over. The moving of a Viceroy in India is a wonderful piece of management. You go to bed in your train, several of your cars go on in advance and meet you at the station, your servants are there behind your chair for a four-course breakfast and even your favourite chair and cushion come along, is on the verandah to meet you. We stay here ten days; the men are out of uniform in white flannels and everything very unceremonious . . . this place is so lovely, really a little cooler, only ordinary August weather. Have just come from flower garden, a riot of sweetpeas, verbena, cornflowers, hollyhocks. It is a glorious summer night; all the verandah lit by electricity, else very primitive. The band of the Gurkhas playing on the lawn. It is a large bungalow, with thatched roof, has a broad verandah all the way round where we lie about in long chairs — views of the Siwalik mountains, distant Himalayas.

Thus, in the pause before the race began, Alice Reading lifted up her eyes to the hills in some apprehension.

I rather dread the house at Simla as I hear it needs so much doing to it. There is a special fund for it, but it seems a hard job to squeeze it out. I don't believe in 100's of servants, no hot water, 8 courses, not one good, magnificent cars, shabby livery.

Yvonne FitzRoy's diary:

At Kalka, the main line terminus, we transhipped into the funniest little train. We climbed slowly, through 100 tunnels, round incredible curves . . . the slope opposite Simla is covered with rhododendron trees, over now except for an occasional scarlet flower, but it must be an amazing sight in full bloom.

The Readings were met by an official reception and went in full panoply, with bodyguard and outriders, to the "heavy, mullioned Victorian-cum-Tudor affair" where they were to live for the next five summers. Sir Grimwood Mears, an old friend from Bar and Washington days, now (1921) Chief Justice of the Allahabad High Court, wrote to Gerald Erleigh about his parents:

> Lady Reading and I had a quiet laugh over the apprehensions at Simla before their arrival. Both your people have had the most amazing success. On arrival at Simla, when everyone recognised they would be desperately tired, they nevertheless shook hands with everyone gathered on the lawn to meet them. This astonished everyone very much. It brought friendliness about at once.

Simla has been much reviled since Kipling's day and most curiously represented on television. It was first discovered as a possible health resort and escape from the heat about 1821. One Major Sir William Lloyd penetrated its virgin forests in May of that year and wrote on his return: "The mountain air seemed to have instilled ether in my veins, and I felt as if I could have bounded headlong down into the deepest glens or sprung nimbly up their abrupt sides with daring ease."[7] By 1831 a French traveller, M. Victor Jacquemont, described it as "the resort of the rich, the idle and the invalid".[8] William Pitt, Baron (later Earl) Amherst (1823–28) was the first Governor-General to take a holiday there. He and his wife returned to Calcutta with "rosy complexions". In Lord William Bentinck's[9] time (1828–35) the government of India bought the district round Simla from a hill rajah, and after that Governors-General came up regularly for holidays.

Sir John Lawrence,[10] a north of India man who found Calcutta particularly uncongenial, decided to take his Council up to the hills with him. He wrote: "I did not go to the hills because I was sick. I did not go there to amuse myself or enjoy myself. I spent five months of the year there because I could serve the Company more laboriously and more effectively than if I had been in the Plains." With his Council under his eye he could drive them as sternly as he drove himself. From that time onwards Simla became the summer headquarters of the supreme government. The Commander-in-Chief and the Governor of the Punjaub also spent the hot weather there with their full administration. Thus the British population was not confined to "hill captains" and grass widows.

In itself Simla is a beautiful place. It is like a garden city scattered up
and down a vast mountain ridge, with tremendous peaks as a background stretching up and away to the permanent snow line. The roads
were then little more than dusty tracks of alarming steepness leading
up or down to houses of very mixed and indifferent architecture
redeemed by their surroundings and cascading gardens. There were
public buildings and a very English church on a wide ledge, and
everywhere dark deodar pines and rhododendrons marched up the
hillside. The deep ravines, scored by waterfalls in the rains, were
efficiently bridged and were inclined to smell of urine in the dry
season, a smell quickly dispelled by the prevailing scent of pine and
wood smoke. The Indian bazaars lay in strips along the hill or tilted
sideways like creepers on the face of a cliff. The majesty and sweep of
the Himalaya must be a discouragement to architects and the gradual
spread of the summer capital over many years tended to diversify
style. Everyone except the great went about in rickshaws by night and
on horses by day. Younger women, on their way to race meetings and
garden parties, hitched up their long skirts and bobbed along on ponies,
picture hats flapping in the breeze, while a *syce* (groom) ran ahead to
hold the pony at the other end. Lady Reading did not enjoy shopping
expeditions in a carriage with attendant Bodyguard and an A.D.C.
clattering behind in a dog-cart. She constantly says how much she
longed to "slip away" into bazaars incognito and she even tried to do
this in Delhi and Calcutta. In Simla it would have been utterly impossible because everything that happened there became common
knowledge in club and bazaar at great speed, owing to the constriction
of society dictated by the lie of the land. As you went along the Mall
you were visible to the bazaars several hundred feet below you, just as
movements below could be spied upon from above. It was a claustro-
phobic life which, combined with the altitude (7,500 feet) tended to
produce *drames des concierges* among the British who regarded Viceregal Lodge as the lodestar, officially and socially.

> "If I was Mrs. What's-her-name
> I would, I would, I would —
> I'd get my husband made a K.
> And see the Viceroy every day,
> I would, I would, I would."

The first few letters Alice Reading writes from her hilltop are a little homesick:

> It is much cooler here, and I cannot tell you what a wonderful spot, I hope you will see it one day not too far distant. Monkeys come by the dozen, and altho' we are high up on the 1st floor, have wire netting at all the windows. We are settling down. I find it tiring, so many people always around one, so little privacy, a great deal of work. I am at work all the morning, some of it interesting, some not, but it's all got to be done.

These monkeys were the handsome, tall grey langurs of the hills, not the organ-grinder type familiar to English people. The langur is a beautiful animal, but as thieving as his brown brother of the plains. The crashing of monkeys through the trees down the hill and their gentle crooning in the branches on a peaceful sunny day are typical Simla sounds.

Mashobra, where the Viceroy had a week-end cottage, lies about six miles from the centre of Simla, in the direction of Tibet. The place was originally a little hill village where buffalo pastured in the hot weather as there was water for them. The name comes from "Maishiara", a collection of buffaloes. Higher and cooler than Simla it had gradually become a small resort, a great place for honeymoon couples and a halt for those who wanted to go further into the unspoilt hills. To get there it was necessary to ride or rickshaw through the long, dark Sanjowlee tunnel and then along a road bordered by an immense precipice falling into a superb valley, many thousands of feet below. It was agony to ride a shying pony to Mashobra but Alice Reading had no such problem:

> I want to describe a week-end place 1¼ hours from here where we have spent Saturday till Monday. The first time since I landed I have been out (even in the garden) without at least *one* Aide. They arrive as soon as I leave my room in the morning and take me there again at night! You can imagine, therefore, we felt like coming out of school. We left by carriage for an hour's ride till we came to a steep hill; here we dismounted. Vice-regal rickshaws each with four men awaited us. We were pushed several miles of winding road, most glorious scenery, till we reached *The Retreat, Mashobra*, perched on a high hill. An enlarged Swiss chalet in brown and gold with wide verandah running round and glorious views, 8,500 feet up. Nothing to be seen but miles of rhododendrons, pines and undergrowth of maiden-hair fern. The house itself *most* primitive, only a cottage, but truly Indian, a magnificent retinue of servants, no lights only smelly oil

lamps and candles, no hot water laid on, iron tubs on zinc floors. Lord
Curzon made the most delightful orchard on the slope of the hills smothered
in cherry trees. Now (May 9th) cherries all ripe under their nets and
greatly appreciated by H.E. The garden ruined by lack of rain, the water
brought to the house in skins by the natives. The servants proceeded in
rickshaws all the way, the coolies carrying most of the luggage on their
heads, the rest slung on mules.

India is so astounding with its contrasts, luxury, squalor, dirt and
magnificence. It's all like a magic carpet, wherever you go in any of our
houses, everything is there in its place on arrival. Great writing tables in
every room and verandah and on lawn under the awning, all stacked with
writing papers, elastic bands, pencils, pins galore. The box of novels by
my bed, my favourite biscuits, Malvern water and milk (from my special
cow) on ice. It is true there is a servant for everything and one man carries
only *one* thing, very exasperating when you are in a hurry but the result
is alright and tends for comfort.

In May an historical interview took place between the Viceroy and
Mr. Gandhi.[11] Gandhi had forbidden a *hartal* (strike) to be held on the
arrival of the Viceroy in India as he was impressed by Lord Reading's
liberal reputation. Yvonne describes how:

Gandhi had arrived in Simla the day before—to a town garlanded and
en fête—albeit good-humouredly so to the last degree. All that afternoon
tom-toms and cries of greeting had floated up to us. But still it seemed
doubtful—would he ever submit to *asking* to see His Excellency? That
evening his letter arrived, delivered through the proper channels and, it
appears, admirably expressed.

Then Alice Reading takes up the tale:

H.E. has had some hard days. Gandhi was here four hours at a stretch
alone with him; for your private ear he had *never* had an interview with
C. (Chelmsford) alone. What the result will be is on the lap of the gods . . .
We were accidentally in the hall when he arrived, had a good view of an
elderly, frail, slim man, climbing stairs with difficulty, dressed all in
homespun, with bare legs. An intelligent face, the eyes of a seer. That was
all we could make out, but by close examination of H.E. we gathered
fuller particulars. A man of eloquence who impressed one by his sincerity,
above all a devout believer in the Simple Life, and the doctrine of ruling
by love. How closely his adherents follow their leader, I should not like
to say! His only food goat's milk and bread, he touches nothing else,
unfortunately we do not encourage goats here so Gandhi had hot water

and with charming courtesy, as H.E. wanted his tea, G. felt he was preventing him. The interviews have followed thick and fast and Gandhi's rickshaw bearers are a familiar feature of my gravel outside, where they squat for hours. They relieve the waiting by playing an eastern game very like throwing of dice only played with stones off my gravel . . .

Both Lord Reading and his wife were caught by the Mahatma's special quality, but they underestimated his power. As time goes on Alice Reading comments with quite obvious regret that he is a "spent force". What she can never have imagined was that he would be assassinated by one of his own race.

In this same letter (early May) she tells of a plunge into what came to mean more to her than any ball or dinner:

I visited the native hospital last week; that was quite the most interesting thing I have done. Firstly the men's and the women's wards then the Purdah [or veiled women's] block. Outside I had to leave the Doctors, Aides and bearers and Sister [Meikle][12] and I, accompanied by the Lady Doctor, went everywhere. I insisted on seeing everything including Out Patients Dept. and Dispensary. This saddened me terribly, mostly little children, so frail, so ricketty, they look worse than European children as their dark skins take a yellow grey tinge and their lips so blue. All of them with their lovely dark eyes and eye-lashes pencilled round with *kohl*. The stories I heard were terrible, the scenes I saw. Such neglect and poverty, above all such superstition, such graft. I went home miserable for it seems almost impossible to fight it. I feel my work in India ought to be directed in that channel.

British society did not interest her so much but she realised that though there were many pretty women, nice clothes, even tiaras, at her parties, Simla (and Delhi) society was not a wealthy society. Nor was there much opportunity for those who composed it to keep in touch with affairs outside India or with the arts and literature. There was no radio or television, or even talking films. Entertainment and culture had to be on a do-it-yourself basis and some of it was very good. What did distress her was the small number of women who took an active part in social work. Those who did do so were very active indeed. Many Englishwomen were desperately homesick and genuinely afraid of stepping out into the seething, fascinating Indian world which Alice Reading herself would have been perfectly ready to explore more closely if she had had time to learn the language and escape from

3

protocol. She seldom met the British in the Districts or in the smaller cantonments, or she would have realised how closely some of them were able to contact Indian life.

The government of India consisted of departments equivalent to ministries at Whitehall — Foreign and Political, Education Health and Lands, Agriculture and Forestry, Law, Finance, Public Works, Commerce, Home — each with a Member of Council appointed by the Viceroy, a Secretary, and a band of lesser civil servants down to clerks and *chaprassees* (messengers). Some of the Members of Council were Indian Civil Service men, some (chiefly Finance and Legal experts) came from outside the service. After the Montagu-Chelmsford Reforms most of the Members of Council were Indians; clerks and *chaprassees* always had been. Army Headquarters was a smaller edition of the War Office, headed by the Commander-in-Chief, with clerks and orderlies at the base of the structure.

The men in jobs at headquarters worked very hard, both civil and military; those on leave were not as numerous as is often supposed, for Simla leave was expensive, but naturally they were the ones most in evidence at parties and picnics. Many of the women raced from party to party to forget the nostalgia for children left at home; many were alone in one small room in a boarding-house or hotel because their health would not allow them to stay with their husbands in the hot weather. Alice Reading greatly liked young people and she instituted special parties for them, not confining her entertaining to official sahibs and memsahibs. Her greatest contribution to Viceregal Lodge was to increase the number of Indian guests, both to meals and to stay. She and her husband knew they were facing prejudice and criticism because they were not of the usual caste from which Viceroy and Vicereine were drawn; they were new to everyone, to the public at home, to the services in India, to the educated Indians, to the Princes and to the commercial community. As for the people of India — the nearest the Viceroy's wife could get to them was in her own hospital which she founded in Simla. She knew, and says, that it was impossible to get nearer, so she visited every patient in every ward twice a week and when she left for ever, these were the people she most sadly missed.

The descriptions of her houses and gardens are better left to her, also her acute impressions of people and situations. Imagine her sitting scribbling away on huge sheets of stiff crested paper, sometimes in the train, sometimes at her table in a briefly-snatched minute before going down to dinner or ball, sometimes in tents, often in bed. Sometimes cold, more often too hot ("no-one knows what heat means till they come to India"), for there was no air-conditioning in those days. Enthusiastic, sympathetic, eager, amused—never discouraged. "I am afraid my letters are so *bald*," she says. It has taken over forty years to discover how mistaken that judgment has proved to be.

CHAPTER III

A Queer Place

"What strange scenes of fine ladies in jampans and liveried coolies!
What groups of beautiful little English children with ayahs and bearers!
What endless picturesqueness of hill tribes with toga-like wrappers!
What women with nose buttons and rings, and spoons and sky blue
    breeches!
Verily, Simla is a queer place!"

Edward Lear's Indian Journal, 19th April, 1874.

THE sequel to Gandhi's interviews with Lord Reading was to force the issue between the Congress Party[1] and the Mohammedan extremists, the brothers Mahommed and Shaukat Ali.[2] At that time there was uneasy alliance in the Congress Party between Muslims and Hindus. The brothers Ali voiced the great discontent in Islamic circles regarding the treatment of Turkey by the British Government at the Treaty of Sèvres.[3] When the Moplah (Mohammedan) rebellion[4] broke out in Malabar in August 1921 and many Hindus were massacred, the leaders of the Congress Party drew back from alliance with the Ali brothers and that was one reason, out of many, why Mr. Gandhi and his colleagues made some gestures of co-operation with the Viceroy. Anti-British sentiment regarded the whole episode as an example of the British policy of "Divide and Rule". The matter ended in a public apology from the Ali brothers for seditious utterances and a guarantee of restraint in the future. Alice Reading writes (June 1st):

> The excitement of the week has been the Gandhi manifesto (or rather that of the brothers Ali) with their promise of non-violence and apologies for language used and inciting to violence in the past. Everyone has been talking of it and H.E's powers of *peaceful* persuasion. Just now a telegram arrived — "Bravo, well played, Sir" — anonymous but it shows the feeling of confidence. The special correspondent of the "Daily Telegraph" happens to be passing through Simla and has travelled through this country from Japan. He told me Rufus's influence is being felt all through

the country already . . . After this a week in bed with the worst attack of sciatica I have ever had which prevented my standing or sitting, so unfortunately the Ball had to take place without me. By yesterday I was able to be carried down and deposited in front of a wonderful stage erected in the ballroom. First came a deputation of our band with a huge bouquet, then dinner, just the whole household, half-a-dozen nice girls for the Aides. My four-tier birthday cake in centre and table all decorated in my honour with mauve flowers. The performance after was a wonderful charade with music, all got up in one week. I was glad to have all this fun and gaiety and young people round me for I felt very sad at being so far away from you all on my birthday.

From her own birthday she goes on to describe the King's Birthday Parade which was held annually on a few square yards in front of the church—the only flat space in Simla other than the polo ground. There were guns, but no horses besides those of the Bodyguard, as these might well have slipped over the edge if there had been any sort of commotion. The troops assembled (one detachment of British troops, one of Gurkhas and a mountain battery on mules), marched past the Viceroy and round the backs of the crowd and into view again like a stage army.

H.E. and I started about 10.30 in semi-state, open britzka like Queen Victoria used to drive in, with postillions in scarlet, gold with white breeches, the Head Coachman (he only drives us and has control of stables and I quail beneath his glance) in scarlet and gold before us. The Bodyguard mounted, A.D.C.s each side of us, altogether a very fine show. It is true I was hoisted into the phaeton and hoisted up by doctor and nurse every time the band of the Seaforth Highlanders played "God Save The King", which rather detracted from the majesty of my presence, but I hope the Indians thought this was part of the pageant as the more helpless you are, the sweller they think you are. It was a lovely sight, a plateau surrounded by pine trees, aforesaid trees manned to the top by Indians with turbans of every colour of the rainbow . . . At night a huge dinner, a great show, all the men in their best and that is wonderful in India. Amongst them several Indians in their native dress but few jewels, those we shall see later on the Rajahs.

June 14th: next week we dine with an Indian Member of Council, as announced—"Their Excellencies will dine with the Hon.ble Khan Bahadur Mian Mahommed Shafi[5] at Inverarm". I am looking forward to this, my first Indian dinner, and particularly as entire Shafi family, consisting of innumerable sisters, aunts and cousins, are all devoted admirers of ours. The men are members of Middle Temple, the women live at Lahore, where the husbands practise as barristers, and only come out of purdah when they visit their parents here at Simla. Lady Shafi only learnt English 12 months ago and unveiled her face.

The Viceregal party went to the Shafi dinner in rickshaws, all the way there and back, and Alice Reading describes the fascination of Simla at night. As the rickshaws wound their way along the hilly paths, the twinkling lights of other rickshaws could be seen like moving necklaces strung along the hillside, above and below. It was, however, an uneasy means of progress. The *jhampanis*,[6] four to each well-sprung bath-chair type vehicle, were hillmen who came in from their villages for the season. It was said that they died young of heart failure and that was easy to believe, as even with a light load they groaned with the effort of pushing up hill and then would tear down the other side, wildly ringing the bicycle bell on the front bar, and straining to hold back the brakeless vehicle. All the senior officials kept permanent teams who had a retaining fee in the winter months. These men were given warm livery and mackintoshes for the rains, and did not fare badly. But the public rickshaw coolies were a sad sight, thin and coughing, in their tattered cotton garments. Their vehicles smelt of *biris*, the native cigarettes, and were liable to harbour bugs. On nights when the rain fell in solid sheets and the lights glowed forth from the Châlet (annexe of the U.S. Club) or some private house, and dance music woke the sleeping monkeys in the trees, the rickshaw coolies huddled in their hooded rickshaws, passing a precious *biri* from hand to hand, not even able to play the endless game of knuckle bones with pebbles which Alice Reading watched when Gandhi's team sat on the gravel outside her window. The *jhampanis* had a tale which they would tell in broken Urdu (as foreign to them as to the passenger) as they trotted along through the bazaars, about evil men who caught *jhampanis* and hung them upside down over a fire till their brains trickled out. For this reason they liked to carry staves which a sympathetic passenger would hide under the rug bound about her knees. As they ran the *jemadar*, or head of team, would sing a strident song to frighten away minor demons, until they came to a waterfall just below the Châlet, dry in summer but roaring in spate in the rains. Here the *jhampanis* would run mute because the fall was haunted by a *churell*, the ghost of a woman who, having died in childbirth, walks with feet turned backwards and drags men to hell. Alice Reading's work must have done something to reduce the number of *churells* in Simla but she came too late to prevent the one at the waterfall beneath the Châlet.

On July 5th she writes about her first Purdah Party.[7] All the functions that were so new in 1921 repeat themselves year by year, but every letter about them has a new facet to describe. Purdah Parties were generally supposed to be a bore but both Alice Reading and Yvonne FitzRoy write of them with enthusiasm and appreciation.

> July 5th: A very full week starting with the Purdah Party which I really think was a huge success. Miss F., the girls [Mary Mond[8] and Doris Robson who had arrived to stay] and helpers were splendid. The Aides were much chagrined when I told them how little they were missed! We had the Hindoo ladies behind a screen in the ballroom with their fruit, sweets, about 50 of them, the other 50 at small tables, but the Hindoos were so afraid of missing anything they continually appeared from behind the screen, had to be shoo'd back.

All the food for the orthodox Hindu ladies had to be carried in and laid on the tables before the party by Brahmin servants, and they had special plates and cups that could be used by no-one else. However, all joined together for the cinema and Her Ex. had especially chosen the films. It was such a pity that no Vicereine could possibly find time to learn any Indian language sufficiently well to hold a conversation. Lady Reading tried to arrange some Hindustani lessons, largely in order to be able to talk to the servants in whom she took a great interest. And she did deplore, in later years, being unable to talk to patients in hospital. The spirit was willing but there was literally no time for lessons.

On June 13th two very remarkable ladies came to visit Alice Reading. They were the pioneers of maternity and infant welfare in India having been, as Yvonne FitzRoy puts it—

> ... plumped down in Delhi by the Government and told to get on with it. With no advice and very little help they have done wonders—during the riots were the only Europeans left in the town and, from a position of considerable danger, have risen to one of perfect security and won the confidence of the poorest and most fiercely conservative people in the world.

Miss Graham and Miss Griffin, for those were their names, were typical of many European women who worked away quietly and without advertisement either in missions or in government employ. They seldom appeared at the Club or in official society. Lady Reading quickly perceived the quality of women of this sort. She never failed to include them in social functions as well as work.

On July 14th the Begum of Bhopal[9] arrived to stay. This famous Indian ruler appears in Lady Reading's letters over and over again. She was one of the outstanding figures of the time, a classic example of the power and honour that comes to an Indian woman in later life when she has achieved her first purpose of child-bearing and rearing. The Begum had three sons and Lord Reading proved to be instrumental in arranging the succession as she wanted it before his Viceroyalty ended.

> July 14th. A full house of visitors staying. Sir John and Lady Maffey,[10] the Begum of Bhopal, her son, Sir Grimwood Mears and a stray man or two, together with the girls [Mary Mond and Doris Robson] compose the house-party . . . The Begum a wonderful old lady, aged 64. Partly purdah, that is to say she is swathed from head to foot, with a piece of tulle just over the eye part. A particularly knowing pair of black eyes take in everything. The rest of her costume consists of a cotton garment, but round her head a half tiara of fine diamonds. Now I know why the Indian ladies asked me to wear my tiara at 4 in the afternoon. She is a shrewd old woman with very advanced ideas on education, emancipation of women, etc. . . . .
>
> The only untoward incident of the week was "Their Exes" were stuck in the new lift miles from the ground floor as lunch was on the table. It was the funniest sight, but not so pleasant an experience. Miss FitzRoy, Smith, the Aides, Mil. Secretary, Comptroller below shouting directions, engineer gone to lunch, and only we, Capt. Leslie and a small lift boy in cage. After a long wait, fortified by fans, smelling salts, hoisted up by a rope, a high ladder arrived and we crept and crawled till we reached *terra firma*, so all was well.
>
> Yesterday I took the Begum to see my '*bête noir*,' the Women's Hospital. She was quite as dissatisfied as I am and we shall now hasten on our plan of campaign for a new Hospital. This morning a wild chase to finish my mail interrupted by plans for a new annexe at Delhi to house the Prince [of Wales]. Stubborn resistance on my part to tack a Swiss châlet on to an Italian building. I carried the day and annoyed the architect.

On July 27th Lady Reading paid the first of many visits to the Convent of Jesus and Mary, which was situated on the far side of Mount Jakko in lovely unspoiled surroundings. This community of nuns ran the largest girls' school in the north of India, for English and European children. The house differed from most of those in Simla, in being architecturally charming, built about 1860. Alice Reading always felt rested and happy with these nuns and Yvonne FitzRoy felt it too and says in her diary:

> The Mothers showed Her Ex. round — and certainly cleanliness and godliness walked beautifully hand in hand, and with it a certain spirit of serene enthusiasm, and lives kept young by their dedication to youth. Not to mention a very evident sense of humour. We finished at the teachers' training school where some of the older girls work, and with an inspection of the kitchen, where open jam tarts cooked by a French sister (to whom, on arrival, the devil appeared in the shape of a monkey!) finally convinced us of our peculiar fitness for the contemplative life!

Alice Reading says that she had such a wonderful welcome from the children that she wanted to hug them. "Everything so restful, so peaceful, I felt like 'going over to Rome'." She immediately invited the whole school (300 of them) to tea at Viceregal Lodge.

By this time the monsoon had arrived and though the mountains were covered in cotton-wool clouds and fungus grew on shoes, books and clothes, the rush of wild flowers and the beauty of tame ones in her garden greatly cheered the Vicereine.

> The best week-end we have had at Mashobra. The place looked too wonderful, with an undergrowth of maiden-hair fern, fresh green ferns and masses of wild flowers, wild lily of the valley, baby orchids, etc. The return Monday morning is always a delight, the rickshaw ride down-hill all the way, the wonderful views over the hills and mountains a continual joy.

She came back to a full programme, a big dinner, a dance for 300 —

> I find these [the dances] less interesting as I sit on the dais and watch the others, only talking to the mighty, but I like my morning's work. To day I have been in an hour's conversation with doctors of Simla seeing how we can save the hospitals which are in a bad pecuniary state. Yesterday, I had the Minister of Education talking over schemes for opening new Health Centres. Tomorrow I open a Sale-of-Work in aid of an Orphanage and so on. I rest all the afternoons, and only re-appear to go for a short drive in my rickshaw, mostly to inspect the gardens, or watch the tennis. I hardly ever leave the grounds as I find the gardens, tennis and view of surrounding mountains more peaceful and alluring than a drive with escort when I have to bow right and left the whole time for miles . . . We are literally in the clouds, but the sunsets are a joy. No-one has seen a sunset till they have seen the sun disappear behind the Himalayas. The

border in the garden is looking wonderful since the rain, hollyhocks, cornflowers, dahlias, salvias, buddleias galore and fortunately I have a charming head-gardener who does not object to cutting, so my sitting-room looks a picture with masses of madonna lilies and huge bunches of every other shade of blossom.

She did not really want the trappings of royalty, but since they were there she assumed them with dignity. It must never be forgotten that not only the eyes of Indian society were upon her, but the jealous eyes from England of those who would have liked to be in her place, and also the eyes of world Jewry who saw in Lord Reading the greatest Jew in English history since Disraeli. Writing to her son on the same day as the above letter, she says, for his and his wife's eyes only:

I am better than I was as regards heart but find climate very trying as am lame with rheumatism, *hear* so badly. It is a great trial (my hearing) particularly as Indians, partly through shyness and partly through soft voices speak in an undertone always, but so far I have had my chief success among the Indians. I hope you won't think it conceited if I say I am a success. I was much amused at a conversation repeated to me the other day. A prominent official said: 'We trembled when we heard the Readings were coming, *Jews, too*. We knew they had the brains but it was the social part we felt so alarmed about, now we have never had such hosts . . .' (so *he* said). I hate repeating all this but Miss F. says she will if I don't, so that's that.

CHAPTER IV

Principalities and Powers

"The Rajput . . . worships his horse, his sword and the Sun,
and attends more to the martial song of the Bard than to
the litany of the Brahmin."

Annals and Antiquities of Rajasth'an
by Colonel James Tod, Vol. I, p. 57.

DURING the years of British rule in India, the sub-continent
came to be divided between British India and the hereditary
states, ruled over by autocratic rulers. British India consisted
of three presidencies (Madras, Bengal, Bombay) and seven provinces:
Punjaub, United Provinces of Agra and Oudh (now Uttar Pradesh), the
North-West Frontier Province, the Central Provinces (now Madhya
Bharat and Maharashtra), Bihar and Orissa, Assam, and Burma. The
presidencies were allotted Governors sent out from England, men
distinguished in public life, and the provinces were governed by senior
members of the Indian Civil Service. The Viceroy reigned over all
with the full title of Viceroy and Governor-General in Council. When
India was still nominally controlled by the East India Company the
Governor-General did not bear the title Viceroy, but when the Crown
assumed the rulership, in 1858, the Governor-General became the
direct representative of the Crown, the personification of the Monarchy.
Hence the protocol and the curtseying which has often provoked
criticism in these more democratic days. There was no such title as
"Vicereine", though it is constantly used by nearly everyone who writes
about the British Raj in India. Curtseying included the Viceroy's wife,
as his Consort, not as representing a Queen. No-one else had any
official right to a curtsey, but the habit was infectious and British
people in doubt at official functions were apt to give way at the knees
at the slightest sign of authority. Indians usually employed their own
forms of salutation, since to make obeisance, in some form or another,
is a custom built into Indian history, a matter of good manners rather
than servility, based on a deeply-rooted hierarchical social structure.

43

The bobs made to the Viceroy and his wife were mere sketches beside the tributes offered to the Princes by their subjects, even those of the highest rank. Or, for the matter of that, the respect shown to a father in an old-fashioned Indian family.

The relationship between the Viceroy and the Indian states was necessarily of great importance. There were 601 of them in all, varying from areas the size of France to that of a smallholder's farm. Their history also varied greatly; several were created by the British, many were the outcome of the disintegration of the Moghul Empire, but some were of extremely ancient and romantic foundation. Their order of seniority under the British Raj rested on relative area and wealth, not on antiquity or ancient lineage. They fell into groups: the Hindu states of Rajasth'an and Maharashtra, the Muslim states and the Sikh states. Mysore, founded by the British from the remains of Tipu Sultan's domains and given to a Hindu ruler, and Kashmir, sold by the East India Company to a Hindu ruler, were territories lying outside the main groups. Forty of the leading states had direct treaty relations with the British Crown and all were the responsibility of the Governor-General and the Political Department, who posted a Resident in each state or group of small states to keep an eye on what was going on. There was no sort of representative government in these states; they were autocracies depending on the personality of the Ruler, whom in extreme cases of misrule, the Viceroy had the power to dethrone. The Montagu-Chelmsford Reforms created the Chamber of Princes, a consultative body without executive power, which met twice yearly in Delhi and Simla. When the Princes gathered for the meetings of the Chamber, they were often guests at Viceregal Lodge. They also stayed there at other times and the Viceroy paid visits to them in return, for sport and discussion of their affairs.

Alice Reading writes many pages about the various rajahs, as she usually calls them. She was ever open to the interest of their several personalities, and noted their beautiful jewels and attractive clothes. India was so new to her that she never quite separated one group or creed from another, or got her terminology correct. But she was unfailingly hospitable and welcoming and fascinated by her return visits. Lord Birkenhead, in his life of Lord Halifax, says that the Princes did not like Lord Reading. It would be fairer to say that he was a man they may have found difficult to place and they must all have immediately realised that he had as subtle a brain as any of them, or of their *diwans*, since in many states most of the brain work was done by the prime minister and not by the Ruler.

The Princes of Rajasth'an were and are unique in that they have a known and chronicled history going back thousands of years. The Rajput and his cousin, the Jat, are descended from Scythian tribes of central Asia who migrated, some to India and others to north Europe, where they appear in history as Goths and Jutes. Many Rajput feudatory customs are exactly similar to our own in Saxon times—for instance, the measurement of land by hide. No-one can claim to be a true Rajput if he does not own at least one hide of land. Only a true Rajput may carry arms and a Rajput does not do manual labour. A Rajput is a great hunter of game, a horseman and a soldier. It can be appreciated that a race of independent barons, to whom the possession of land was almost a religion, would feel at home with a similar type of long-established baron and land-owner who happened to hold the overlordship of their country. Lord Reading, a lawyer and a townsman, they regarded with some caution, until they came to know and trust him.

H.H. of Alwar[1] appears frequently in Lady Reading's letters, for she much enjoyed his conversation and visits, though she describes him as "uncanny". He was of so evil a character that he remained beyond her imagination. The Marquis de Sade and all his habits were not customary reading or hearing for a woman, especially so sheltered a woman as she was. She writes in July, 1921:

His Highness of Alwar, young, cultured (as to education), voluble, not difficult to entertain, which is my first thought as they always sit on my right at lunch and dinner. He is gorgeous to look at, came down to dinner in a brocade coat stiff with embroideries of pink roses. An old rose velvet cap (not turban) with magnificent ruby ornament. He varied it last night by wearing a striped velvet coat and the most magnificent necklace of emeralds. He is a mighty hunter. He has brought his Prime Minister and innumerable secretaries, typewriters, etc., with him. The place swarms with them.

Though the Rajputs were not at the top of the priority list for precedence, there was no disputing the supremacy of the Maharana of Mewar (Udaipur), at that time a very old man, known as the Sun of the Hindus. It was fascinating to visit Rajasth'an and there will be many descriptions of these visits in Lady Reading's letters. The atmosphere recalled the *Song of Roland* or pages from Malory's *Morte d'Arthur*.

The Rajput princes were accustomed to adapting themselves to an alien invader. In their many thousands of years in India they had to contend with numerous waves of Islamic conquest, culminating in the Moghul dynasty. They had, in the break-up of that dynasty, to fight the Mahrattas. Sometimes they were unconquered, sometimes they compromised, all the time they maintained their special character and customs. At the dawn of their history they were alien invaders themselves. In token of this, an aboriginal Bhil takes a principal part in the initiation ceremony of the Ruler of Mewar; he applies the *thika* or "caste mark" to the new king, since the aboriginal tribes were the real Indians long, long ago before Rajputs, Brahmins, Muslims, the British, the Congress Party or anybody who has power in India to-day.

In addition to entertaining the princes, the Viceroy received visits from time to time from the Presidency and provincial governors who arrived with staff and servants. These visits were also reciprocated. One of the first to come to Simla in 1921 was Sir Harcourt Butler from the United Provinces (now Uttar Pradesh). Alice Reading was rather nervous about his visit but after he left he sent her a bread-and-butter letter which gave her great pleasure. She quotes from it:

> "I had heard great things of your Excellencies, but feel, like the Queen of Sheba, '*the half was not told me*'. When I had seen 'the meat of his table, the sitting of his servants, and the attendance of his Ministers and their apparel', there was no more spirit in me." He goes on to say he will try to make us comfortable when we come but he can only give us "brass for gold".[2] As he has the most luxurious Government House in India, you can imagine I was pleased.

On August 10th the whole Viceregal house-party set off for a return visit to Sir Harcourt at his hill station, Naini Tal. On August 13th she writes from there:

> Here we are at the top of another mountain after 24 hours' journey. The journey was rather wonderful coming down right from the clouds. Half-way down we found our wonderful train looking smarter than ever as my sitting-room has been re-dressed in putty colour with great vases of pink gladioli. The night was unbearable in spite of sleeping draught, electric fans, etc., and rather trying to scramble up to salute of guns and acres of scarlet carpet at 7.45 a.m. A big breakfast in train where the judges, officers, etc., joined us and we changed from broad to narrow-gauge railway where a surprise awaited us in the shape of another royal train, smaller, but even more attractive than the other, with a boudoir all in pale

green and white moiré for me, all the bath-rooms with shower-baths, etc. We reached our train journey's end in mist and fog. Six motors awaited to take us up to Naini Tal. Unfortunately the fog spoilt the view, but we had visions of one waterfall after the other, masses of the palest green fern and bushes of wonderful apricot lily-like flowers which grow wild here. Another Scottish fortress, with a group of gracious hosts, a carrying-chair; Dr. and Nurse and bed is all I remember for some hours till various members of our party straggled in to inform me of a lovely golf-course, a swimming-bath, a lake with fresh trout (one of which was promptly caught for my dinner) and various other attractions.

H.E. has his secretaries, shorthand-typists, etc. up here. No-one ever saw such a move as we do, everybody seems to take everything. When I tell you I had a vision of the girls' gramophone changing trains, you can imagine what it means, but there are 70 servants with us to do it besides a special gentleman whose only duty all the year is to look after luggage.

On return to Simla she writes:

I rested and read and tried to forget the cares and responsibilities of a Vicereine. Our visit was all too short for we were recalled after six days. The part I enjoyed consisted of the lovely grounds, cinder paths with high banks of maiden-hair fern and mauve orchids on either side. Sir Harcourt, who is gouty, and I who am shaky, had rickshaws so I saw all the lovely grounds with little exertion. We had a pleasant time, tho' I felt quite happy to get back to Viceregal Lodge and all my work. We have a very busy month before us with relays of visitors, 3 more Governors, dinners for them galore, a big bazaar for the Y.W.C.A., etc.

This is the lighter side of India. The problems are grave and wax bigger each week. H.E. is working far too hard but the situation requires it. We anxiously await telegrams but by the time this reaches you I hope the sun will be shining. The burdens are heavy to bear, one needs all one's courage, all one's optimism, all one's faith.

She is alluding to the bad news about the Moplah insurrection which had cut short the visit to Naini Tal. This finally resulted in the arrest of the Ali brothers who had fermented trouble in this fanatical Muslim sect, far away in south India.

This first Simla season ended with the opening of the Legislative Assembly and the visit of "Pussyfoot" Johnson:[3]

Friday we had a great meeting in the evening of all the Indian members of the Legislative Assembly, starting with a reception. Rufus and I stood on the steps of the throne and shook hands with every member as he filed past. Some of the costumes quaint, some gorgeous. One Deputy arrived in an overcoat, it took two Aides to make him part with it in the cloakroom as he insisted he might feel cold, but I think there was method in his madness. I have often longed for an overcoat myself on monsoon nights.

Next day the opening of Parliament, quite a fine show with State carriages, outriders and cavalry escort. H.E. looked wonderful against the panelling of the New Parliament House which made a splendid background. His speech was applauded continually and we had a great reception on our return. Meanwhile the situation everywhere has eased a bit. Malabar is simmering down and the conviction has penetrated far and wide that H.E. is not to be trifled with.

September 14th: have been busy receiving Indians who are up here for Legislative Assembly. One dear old man paid me a visit yesterday and gave me half a lakh of rupees (£3,600) towards my Indian hospital (a dream of the future) and a promise of another half-lakh in the future. You can imagine how delighted I was.

On September 21st Lady Reading describes their first Investiture, a function which was to happen many times again. There is a most human and characteristic touch in this letter about the banners that hung on each side of the throne:

> . . . on one side a huge, pale blue banner of the Crown of India, on the other the dark blue of the Viceroy with inscriptions of gold. I had the banners taken down earlier in day and *ironed*, my friends will appreciate this! And removed pots of crimson and blue fuchsias which the gardeners thought suitable adjuncts to scarlet uniforms. I substituted salvias.

> September 29th: the Pussyfoot Johnson lunch, he on my right and every ear turned my way for fear I should curry favour with him by telling him I had never drunk a glass of wine in my life. A very human old thing. He was not a great success on the platform or else it was a very wet night, but even Simla could not assimilate: "It is a very *wet* night to address you on a *dry* subject." I hear there were yawns galore.

The days drew near their departure and the glorious after-rains weather made up for long weeks of damp:

> The monsoon is over, the weather lovely, clear, champagne-like, with a hot sun, such wonderful dark blue nights with starry skies. The horizon looks clearer in a political sense. The Moplahs, if not at rest, are not at their most active. The Ali brothers are being tried, so far it has caused little excitement. Still, when we have nothing else we can always fall back

Alice, Countess of Reading, by Glyn Philpot, R.A.

Rufus Isaacs, first Earl of Reading, Viceroy of India,
by Philip de Laszlo, R.A.

on Afghanistan. So the days fly, and six months have passed, very full busy days, some grave, some gay. Soon our time at Simla is coming to an end, we leave for Kashmir and holiday.

Yvonne FitzRoy must have the last word, describing a dance on October 2nd:

It was colossal! Reverend gentlemen, renowned hitherto for their eloquence in the Legislative Assembly or the Council of State— or for the dignity of their demeanour during interviews with the Viceroy—raced the length of the ballroom on cushions—danced in solitary defeat blowing gold bugles—tore round the room in teams of four to the strains of John Peel—bleated like sheep or roared like lions, and laughed without ceasing, only less I am glad to think, than their Exes. Since then they (the guests) have enlarged, on the telephone, on the road, to each other and all and sundry, that never in their lives have they had such an evening.

And this in a house where six months ago we were solemnly assured that it was quite—*quite*—impossible to be anything but a model of positively alarming decorum. What we all said when we arrived (and got laughed at) has indeed been conclusively proved. Nothing is impossible, it depends only on two people—the host and the hostess.

CHAPTER V

Seven Cities

"Dilli dur ast — It is a far cry to Delhi."

Indian Proverb

DELHI is a beleaguered city, beleaguered by ghosts who can be felt almost as a physical force in all of the seven areas where, at one time or another, a conqueror has built his forts and palaces and then gone his way. At the time of the building of the eighth city there were many who repeated an old legend that the eighth would be the last and that whoever built it would lose it. But this is no new legend in Delhi; it is exactly what happened to all the previous rulers who lived and lorded it in the past. The very earliest Delhi of all was a Hindu kingdom under Prithviraj, a Rajput. He lost it, and his life, in 1192. After that it became a Muslim city till 1947 when the Hindu Raj took it back again. The oldest preserved site is out on the south-west, the city of Qutb-u-din Aibek, a Turkestan slave, founder of the so-called "Slave Dynasty"; the remains of the next three cities lie in the same area, Siri, Tughlaqabad, and Jehan Panna. After that the rulers and builders moved nearer to the Jumna and Firozabad, Indrapat (where the Purana Khila, the Old Fort, stands) and Shajahanabad are all close together. The last-named is the seventeenth century city of the Emperor Shah Jehan and still a busy, flourishing place. In the Readings' time this was the centre of government though Viceregal Lodge lay some distance away on the other side of the Ridge that runs to the north-west of New Delhi, the seat of government to-day. The whole area is about six hundred square miles and every inch of it impregnated with the blood and bones of the past.

In 1911 the capital of India was moved by decree from Calcutta to Delhi, the logical outcome of Disraeli's imperial policy in the nineteenth century. Until the new city could be ready, the Government and the Viceroy dwelt in rather charming camp conditions. Viceregal Lodge stood in large grounds and was really no more than a vast bungalow of vaguely Palladian design with little room for guests and staff. These lived in large, permanent tents, with solid floors and fire-places. The Ridge was visible from the grounds and the little fort on it where the few women and children who escaped from the centre of Delhi in the Mutiny sheltered in the hot weather of 1858. It was from the Ridge that John Nicholson[1] directed the relieving force, and he died at the Kashmir Gate below the hill. In order to shop or go to church or to sight-see, it was necessary to pass through the Kashmir Gate, a most evocative portal which led on to James Skinner's[2] church and the Arsenal where the British garrison blew themselves up rather than surrender. There were English ghosts among all the Hindu, Central Asian, Mahratta and Afghan spectres, especially on the Ridge in the evening, and in an officers' quarter over the main gate of the Red Fort where even the stolid garrison gunners in the twentieth century felt uneasy. Nowadays all the Delhis are joined by suburbs and roads but in 1921 the area was a jumble of graveyards, tombs small and great, and stretches of open country where sacred peacocks trailed their tails in the dust and sometimes a herd of blackbuck could be seen leaping against the empty sky. Shah Jehan's[3] Red Fort and the Jumma Masjid, the Great Mosque, dominated the walled city as they do still. The outer wall of the Fort falls sheer into the plain of the Jumna; the river is now distant and not flowing under the walls as it used to do when the Moghul Emperors gave *darshan*,[4] showing them-selves to the people, on a little platform standing out from the main battlement. Beyond the city lies the Purana Khila, with Humayon's[5] mosque and library, and not far away, his magnificent tomb, surrounded by trim gardens. Further west the city of the Tughlaq dynasty lay (in those days) in a series of crumbling, roofless walls where shepherds pastured their goats and sometimes Gujars, gypsies in bright-coloured clothes, camped there, guarded by packs of yelling dogs. The Qutb, with its amazing minaret and ancient iron pillar, completed the circle north again. All these places were favourite haunts for picnics, day and night. Tourists were few and came only as guests of British residents. The karela, the wild jungle vine, was kept at bay — no more. There never was such a nostalgic, beautiful, haunted and dramatic place as Old Delhi. Only the new city was then lifeless and foundation-high.

On the way from Simla the Viceregal party paid a visit to the Maharajah of Kashmir.[6] They repeated this in 1924 under happier circumstances; this first visit was also their first experience of princely hospitality and state and Alice Reading writes at great length about it.

Her letter is quoted in full in the second Marquess of Reading's life of his father. On her second visit she had absorbed the real atmosphere of India, could see through the surface panoply and write with perception of more lasting beauties. On the way back to Delhi, one small incident bears her individual stamp and recalls a scene from some old German fairy tale. In camp at Domel she writes:

> I went for a little walk and met a group of wood-cutter's children and presented them each with a small coin. By the time I returned the news was all over the village and everyone told the Police Inspector: "The Lady Sahib scattered silver as she walked"!

She writes to her son and daughter-in-law on November 2nd from Delhi:

> We arrived here two days ago, are now very busy settling down. I am delighted with the alterations I planned during our short stay last April . . . It all looks so clean and cool with wonderful outlook on to a marble piazza and gardens with yew hedges and flower beds. Beyond that rows and rows of tents for guests and staff . . . I love the house here, it is like a monster villa at Monte Carlo with its marble balustrades, cactus and white shining balcony, with flowers, palms everywhere.

On November 7th Lord Reading opened the second session of the Chamber of Princes. Yvonne FitzRoy writes:

> They sit in a chamber of the temporary Secretariat, rather a handsome, panelled oval room with H.E.'s chair of state at one end and galleries overhead. Bikaner,[7] Gwalior,[8] Alwar, Kapurthala[9] and the Jam Sahib[10] were perhaps the most familiar figures, and Gwalior was arrayed in an elegant pink hat not unlike those one associates with a Dresden shepherdess.

Her Ex. describes how Maharajah Alwar

> nearly always wears gloves for fear he should touch anything made of cowskin (the gloves are of chamois or silk), he holds the cow so sacred, but goes nearly mad when he sees a dog and writes beforehand when paying a visit asking all dogs to be removed. Report says he kills them when he sees them so you can imagine the Aides' mongrels are chained up.

It was affectation for Alwar to make such a fuss as he was quite a minor Rajput, descended from the elder son of the house of Amber in the fourteenth century. The descent deviated considerably through paths of adoption and illegitimacy, and the State of Alwar did not take shape until late in the eighteenth century. In the 1920's the Maharajah's fads were a source of some smiling behind the hand among his peers.

The Readings gave large dinner parties for the Princes, and for the members of the Legislative Assembly and the Council of State. These took place in the ballroom, prepared for the visit of the Duke of Connaught[11] in 1920. It was a beautifully proportioned room with tall eighteenth-century windows and five crystal chandeliers, brought from Belvedere,[12] the house where the Viceroy stayed in Calcutta. On all occasions Alice Reading designed the flower decorations herself, for which she had a great gift. Masses of crimson roses, or banks of sweet peas the length of the huge table relieved the almost barren simplicity of the room, and behind each chair stood a *khitmatgar* (table servant) in long white coat with crimson cummerbund, each with his hands raised to his forehead in salute till the Viceroy took his seat, and the meal began. When the time came for the ladies to leave, they rose and followed the Vicereine to the end of the table and each had to make a solo curtsey in the doorway before leaving. Meanwhile the Viceroy stood at the head of the table and bowed to each lady in turn as she rose, sometimes unsteadily, from the floor. Lord Minto[13] (1905–10) introduced this custom which could be very impressive if well done.

We have a Rajah staying here now,

writes Lady Reading in November,

the Mehtar of Chitral.[14] He sat next me at lunch with his interpreter and had ridden 135 miles on horseback to get a train and then travelled four days to come here. When I said (interpreted) how good it was of him to come so long a journey, he said in his *floweriest*, "*No* journey was long if your Excellency was at the end of it." This interpreted by a blushing Secretary before a table full of guests!!! My feelings! At night we dined in the big ballroom, a table decorated with red roses and all the Viceregal plate . . . two days ago Colonel Bury[15] sat next to me at dinner, straight from the Mt. Everest expedition. They got to 20,000 feet and he told me found rats there who stole their biscuits from beside their beds, goodness knows what they, the rats, feed on in that altitude. They seem very satisfied with the observations they have made but were too late in the year starting as snow made greater heights impassable. They lost one member from heart failure. The mules were a dead failure . . .

One pleasant afternoon was when H.E. and some of the giddy ones went to Meerut Races.[16] I stayed at home, rested, and we took a picnic tea to a disused mosque. Next to it a tomb of former Moghul ruler his wife and son. The son was so cruel he was known as "the Bloody", but when he came to the throne he bought penance from all his victims' families and had the receipts put in a chest at the head of his tomb so that he might present them when called to judgement! The whole of Delhi is studded with old mosques, burial places and tombs, and as all are sacred ground not touched, look uncared for and broken-down condition, but I love the place.

The Chamber of Princes reached the end of its session on November 11th and "we had a last big party for the Princes", says Alice Reading on November 16th,

> At their request I went to their Council Chamber to hear the last debate; they put an armchair next to H.E.'s throne, the first time a woman has ever been on the floor of the House. In the afternoon His Highness of Alwar presented himself for a farewell visit to H.E. and as nothing would do but he must say goodbye to me, I had an hour's talk and tea alone with him. He is great on the transmigration of souls and is altogether the most interesting of the Rajahs, as to brains.

Life was not only confined to festivities and entertaining, there was work to do as well. Yvonne FitzRoy notes the first meeting to discuss the amalgamation of the various charitable funds under one head, the All India Fund, a meeting of the Lady Chelmsford League,[17] another of the Minto Association.[18] Time was found for drives to Okhla, the junction of the Agra Canal and the Jumna, a cool, green oasis reached by a fine seventeenth-century bridge; to the Purana Khila, described by Yvonne:

> ... the walls are beautiful, and except for the greater perfection and elabora-tion of the arched gateways and the graceful columned watchtowers, very like the battlemented walls of mediaeval England. The mosque, which is in perfect preservation, is open on one side to a wide view over the plain and the Jumna. It is a wonderful building, inlaid with coloured stones, marble, slate and tiles.

Meanwhile, Lord Reading went down to Bombay to welcome the Prince of Wales to India. Gandhi decreed a *hartal* which was meant to be non-violent but ended in riots which were not directed against Europeans but became communal. On November 24th Alice Reading sums up:

A singularly uneventful week composed of Committees and indigestion. We are just marking time till we start on our journey to Benares, which I am so anxious to see. The Maharajah is putting a lovely guest house at our disposal, thus we break the journey to Calcutta. He is also bringing us in state in barges down the river, having a banquet and fireworks and a garden party in our honour.

I love Delhi. It is a wonderful place full of dust and monuments, mosques and plots. The very dust you eat tastes of "Great Moghul". The usual thing is to take picnic tea out with you or, as it is called here, have "Tea on a Tomb". All the bazaar is tremendously non-co-operative and pro-Gandhi, such a contrast to Simla, but it is a fascinating spot and must be treasure trove to archaeologists. I hear the new Palace is supposed to be ready in four years, just in time for me to get it ready for my successor!

Yesterday the Hardinge College.[19] After Christmas I have to unveil a statue to her and give an address! (Ah, woe is me!!) to inaugurate the new buildings. One hostel for women is to be called after me and I am now drawing up an agonized appeal to various wealthy Rajahs to help me in my praiseworthy efforts to gather together a few lakhs of rupees to complete the building . . . It's all very well done, Mahommedans, Eurasians, Brahmins and Hindoos all seem to live happily together, only do not share meals. There is a big hospital attached to it, a large training centre for Indian nurses and my appeal embraces this and my pet project, the Simla hospital for Women and Children.

We were very glad to welcome H.E. from Bombay. He was delighted with the Prince's success, he is warming hearts wherever he goes.

November 27th: the Gaekwar of Baroda[20] and suite have come on a visit; the Prince has just left him so we shall hear how it all went off. I have spent the morning trying to instil into the architects and builders some idea of colour and comfort in the Prince's house. Indian furniture is terrible, every drawer sticks and it is varnished till a jelly-like compound adheres everywhere, a great source of trouble to me.

The Gaekwar of Baroda, a cheery soul, very easy to entertain. I find one touch of indigestion makes the whole world kin. We have chummed up tremendously over Karlsbad and our little Marys, and last night when everyone else was feasting, munched our pounded chicken together, the best of friends. He wore a long, white satin coat stuck all over with orders, most of them reproduced in precious stones. On his head a little hat made of old rose velvet which I coveted as a toque.

The Gaekwar of Baroda, Sayaji Rao, one of the three leading Mahratta rulers, had been selected by the Government of India after his predecessor attempted to poison the Resident by putting diamond dust in his food. (The trial of Malhar Rao Gaekwar conducted by a commission of three Englishmen and three Indians in 1875 ended in acquittal, but he was deposed.) Sayaji Rao, ably educated and trained by a Mahratta Prime Minister, became one of the most enlightened rulers in India. He was the model for the Maharajah in Louis Bromfield's book, *The Rains Came*. He died in 1939.

Mahrattas were originally cadets of the Rajput clans who moved south into the Deccan in the seventeenth century pillaging and carving out kingdoms for themselves. Over the centuries they achieved great power and very individual characteristics. By the end of the eighteenth century, they had nearly founded an empire based on Delhi and the ruins of the Moghul dynasty. They also came near to defeating the English, indeed might have done so had not the Mahratta Wars been largely directed by Arthur Wellesley, the future Duke of Wellington. Lacking the grace of Rajputs, Mahrattas have qualities all their own, one of the most conspicuous being a sense of humour. Of all Brahmins, the Mahratta Brahmin is the most subtle. At the height of their power the Brahmins organised warfare and statesmanship with skill and discipline. If they could only have been faithful to each other, they might be ruling India to this day.

Yvonne's comment on the Gaekwar's visit:

The Gaekwar to luncheon—a most agreeable man who, having rashly confided his troubles to Her Ex., was immediately dieted with great severity.

CHAPTER VI

Sacred and Secular

"Thorā khānā aur Banarās rahnā — A little to eat and
to live at Benares." (The wish of a pious Hindu)

Indian Proverb

ON the way to Calcutta they paused at Benares — Kashi — the centre and inspiration of orthodox Hinduism. Mr. Niraud Chaudhuri[1] points out that Hinduism is not the correct term for the religion of the Hindus, the latter meaning a people who inhabit Hind. The word for their religion is *Santana Dharma*, the Eternal Way. In that Way are many subways, or byways, amongst them the way of Rivers, which have a sacramental connotation all over India. The Ganges is not by any means the only sacred river. Burning ghats are to be found on other river banks. However, Benares is, as it were, a Cathedral City of the Way, and the Ganges at this point is running at great strength, so during the centuries immense temples and other sacred buildings have grown up on the banks. The city stands in the centre of a fertile and heavily populated part of India, a part first developed by the invading Aryans who came across Central Asia from Europe. Since it is an ingrained custom among western people to describe the religion of the Hindus as Hinduism, the term will continue to be used in this book.

The Readings expected trouble at Benares because they associated Hinduism with Mahatma Gandhi, but Benares was never a principal centre of his influence. He said himself: "Our prayer for others ought never to be 'God! Give them the light thou hast given to me!' but: 'Give them the light and truth they need for their highest development'." Be that as it may, the Viceregal party had a glad surprise. There were ovations everywhere they went which so encouraged the Viceroy that he insisted on going right into the heart of the city in a small open car with two of his staff. The police had said they would need reinforcements of at least 400 if he did so but, as it turned out, he was quite unprotected and received everywhere with friendliness and many garlands.

Alice Reading's letter from Benares is disappointing. The ivory carriage she rode in, the silver one that carried the Viceroy, the Maharajah's[2] jewels, impressed her more than a voyage down the Ganges on the State barge, huge effigies of horses at the helm, a silver throne on the prow—unused because of the heat.

> The Ganges wonderfully interesting. A perfectly smooth, broad stream— at short intervals long flights of steps or *ghats* and every man, woman and child bathing in its sacred waters or washing their garments. At times an almost naked corpse as not enough money to buy sufficient wood; at other places an opulent column of smoke.

Hinduism is a pervading experience and requires time and, above all, knowledge, to assimilate. Yvonne FitzRoy realised Benares much more vividly. She was deeply interested, baffled, thoughtful and a little uneasy:

> It is an amazing story that is told by that great sweep of water and by the unchanged people who live their lives of worship on its banks. And it seems to be to-day as remote as ever from alien influence. The beauty of Benares is manifest, but its spirit eludes the Englishman of to-day as it eluded, in another sense, the violence of its Mahommedan conquerors 400 years ago.

Calcutta had a special appeal for Lord Reading because of the romance of his first visit there as ship's boy on the *Blair Atholl* (1,777 tons) in 1876. He elected to do this in order to escape from the family fruit business which had no appeal for him. He had refused to sail as an apprentice for that would have tied him down for two years. As a member of the ship's crew he would be free to leave her when he chose. It was on this voyage that he knocked out a bullying bo'sun and won for his shipmates the right to bake their biscuits and make them easier to break, so that the weevils could be destroyed before consumption. Rufus Isaacs was an extremely tough, active man, by no means only the urbane city lawyer that some of his colleagues supposed him to be. He and his wife gave of their best to Calcutta for they felt that the business community, immensely rich and well-organised, still considered themselves aggrieved ten years after the change of capital to Delhi. The educated Indians still resented the partition of Bengal in 1909. Alice Reading liked seeing shops and streets again and enjoyed meeting unofficial people with interests outside the world of Army, Civil Service and Government.

Government House, built by Marquess Wellesley,[3] ceased to be the Viceregal residence after the supreme Government moved to Delhi. It was then handed over to the Governor of Bengal. So the Readings found themselves driving up to Belvedere:

The house is high and white and cool,

says Yvonne,

has grey marble floors and really good pictures . . . it was originally the country home of Warren Hastings, and has since been added to; is a fine three-storied erection with two great flights of steps leading up to the columned entrances back and front, which the Bodyguard adorn very effectively. The furniture is a mighty improvement on Simla; there is a beautiful ballroom, drawing-room and a banqueting hall.

Her Ex., as all her staff affectionately called her, sat down on December 6th to write to her son:

I will not dwell on our separation. God has been so good in keeping us all; I must not grizzle, but I would love to see you all, to go down that wing to the nursery and see three little yellow heads.[4] Close on Christmas I am writing this at 7 at night with all doors, windows open, masses of tuberoses on my desk and so hot I am literally in a Turkish bath. Am supposed to be resting for our first ball here tonight, 900, an Investiture first. We start with the State Lancers!! I have not danced for years. Have got both my knees bandaged like a race-horse to be able to get through as have such terrible rheumatism always, but *vogue la galère*! Was delighted you remembered our wedding day, so was H.E. Thirty-four years of unbroken harmony, each year drawing the bonds of sympathy, love and good comradeship tighter is a record! We might well apply for the Dunmow Flitch!

December 12th, 13th: Mrs. Ronnie Greville[5] arrived yesterday, very moist, *very* chatty and a game sportsman as she only arrived at 5.30 and sat down with us (100) to dinner at 8.15. We dined in the supper room at one large table, a daring innovation of mine, justified by the result. All Calcutta applauded my long table with silver cups and enormous cabbage roses, flanked by the white balcony that runs round the room, with tall palms all round. Four nights ago we gave our first entertainment, an Investiture, followed by Ball to 1,000 guests. We made a great show with all the regalia on. I don't know what Calcutta thought but one lady gave audible vent to her feelings by an exclamation — "Anyway, she knows how to walk"!!!

Yesterday I had one of my most interesting experiences. The University

Women of India gave me a lunch. So well done, so amusing. Each university, Calcutta, Lahore, London, Oxford, Cambridge, Edinburgh, spoke for itself, its own. The woman one side of me had a son who had been to Rugby, Balliol, was now at Bar [Gerald Erleigh had also been at all three,] so we "got together" directly. The sweet cases were mortar boards, the name cards quill pens, all so well done, so refreshingly interested and eager the company, a thing one misses in India where most things seem an effort. I made a long speech outlining my hospital scheme which was so warmly welcomed they formed a committee at once to beg, borrow or steal funds.

I think Calcutta agrees with me better than Simla or Delhi, which is a pity as I am only here three weeks to a month during year. We are full of our own affairs — is Gandhi going to call a '*hartal*' now the Prince has been received? What Dodds[6] will have to tell us when he arrives this week from Afghanistan? Not to speak of all the old gentlemen I am trying to lure into my net and give me lakhs of rupees.

I have been very lucky; on my visit to the Dufferin Indian Women's Hospital I asked to see the nurses' quarters and was told they had no recreation or sitting-room. The next day I had the cheque for it from a neighbouring Maharajah on condition it should be called the Lady Reading Room. To-day Infant Welfare Centres, crèches, milk distribution through the bazaars and city where, in spite of much talk of unrest and not wise to go about in Viceregal cars, I had a splendid welcome. Hundreds of poor little sick kiddies and their mothers and a sick Indian kiddy is one of the saddest sights on earth, dark grey lead colour and legs the size of my fingers.

A Purdah Party of over 150, such lovely saris and jewels and such lovely faces.

Calcutta is a magnificent city of parks, gardens and ornamental waters and splendid buildings. We are out of Calcutta, next to the Zoo, where we hear the lions and the tigers roar. A lovely garden, such fern and palm houses and thousands of giant maiden-hair ferns. It is still so hot I am sitting at 9 p.m. with all windows open. We have to sleep under mosquito nets — such bites!

The Court was great fun. I thought the whole time of Barrie's *A Kiss For Cinderella*[7] and did so wish some of them would *prance* in and wave at me. We arrived at 9.45, were met by Lord and Lady Ronaldshay,[8] all the Aides in their super-best, which is very fine indeed. His Ex. in Privy Councillor's dress, I in a brand new flesh-coloured satin covered with mother-of-pearl embroidery and my best tiara. 'Tis true the papers said I looked wonderful in mauve with Brussels lace and many diamonds!! But such is fame and a male news editor!

Calcutta has a very critical population, mostly people who have made a great deal of money and pride themselves on knowing what's what, but it is very pleasant to be in a big town again and meet all sorts and conditions of people. I much prefer my work to the social side which is intensely fatiguing.

The Readings did not stay in Calcutta to present the King Emperor's Cup at the Races on Boxing Day, as the Prince of Wales was due to arrive for Christmas and it was felt that the Governor of Bengal ought to have the privilege of being sole host to Royalty. Alice Reading writes on December 20th to her son:

> Tonight we have our last dance in Calcutta, rather an ordeal as H.E. and I are very anxious. These are troubled times. It is very difficult to smile and put a good face on things when one's thoughts are certainly not at the dinner table or in the Ballroom. I have certainly felt better here and am sorry to leave for some things. I do think I have made good here, particularly amongst the workers, hospitals, schools and hostels. I like that work best, shall never care for the purely social part.

The "troubled times" to which Alice Reading refers in her letter of December 20th, chiefly concerned the Prince of Wales' visit. He was due in Calcutta at Christmas and though both the Readings assumed in public that the visit was going to be a great success, the memory of troubles in Bombay was with them. Lord Reading carried the whole responsibility for the Prince's safety.

The Treaty with Afghanistan marked the final settlement of the Third British-Afghan War which had been fought out in 1919. The Treaty was signed in November by Sir Henry Dodds.

On the last day of the Calcutta visit, Yvonne FitzRoy notes in her diary:

> Our time here has been so crowded, it seems incredibly short. It has, though, been a long strain for Her Ex. and no easier for the political background at the moment. But I think she would feel rewarded for all it has cost her in strength and effort if she could hear, as we do, something of what Calcutta has to say of her. Not only social Calcutta but working Calcutta and the poor Indian for whom Calcutta works. Neither have there been the ordinary civilities addressed as in duty to her entourage, but something far more spontaneous and so unanimous from every source which she has touched personally that even the pride of a Staff very critical of appreciation has been gratified! And often and often people have said to me, "You don't know the good she has done", and they mean not only amongst the European community but amongst Indians of every

class. Rumour runs through the bazaars like a flame and attains a significance hardly realised in England.

Alice Reading herself writes in the train on the way to Bikaner:

December 28th. We reached Delhi safely. I was delighted to be back with my nice house and garden tho' Calcutta much more amusing and gay. The garden looks wonderful, hollyhocks much taller than I am, the herbaceous border a blaze of colour and all for Christmas! Early on Christmas morning a most lovely Bokhara carpet was brought in to me from the entire Staff. Boxing Day we had a children's party and the mothers came too, from the Viceregal Estate. We had a clown and Father Christmas. They ended up with games and dancing to the band.

I had the best present for Xmas, 2 lakhs of rupees from one of the Maharajahs (a lakh here is worth about Rs. 100,000). Besides this I had half-a-lakh in Simla, and in Calcutta they gave me nearly another half-lakh in smaller sums, making over 20,000 altogether. As I had bought a house and 4 acres of ground in Simla and had to pay for it in January, I was very happy about it all. [The money of course was for her hospital, as were the house and grounds.] People were wonderful to me about it in Calcutta. I began talking to an Indian about my hospital; he said times were bad; I said that I knew, but sick women and children could not wait. Next morning he sent me a bouquet and two bonds for £500 each as a first instalment, and to tell me he was so struck by what I had said he meant to send me again and again. So I shall get my Simla hospital by next spring. When I think how difficult it is at home to sell guinea tickets even for a concert or a dance, I marvel at all the wealth here tho' times are really bad.

We are very relieved that all went well with the Prince's visit to Calcutta. It was an anxious moment till the cables came in but he really had a wonderful reception without any disturbing element.

She did manage to get all the money needed for her charitable schemes, and she is always grateful and says so without imputing ulterior motives to the givers as a more cynical character might have done. It was just this quality of direct unsuspicious belief in the best in human nature that made her acceptable to givers who certainly had ulterior motives, but many generous motives as well. So much is said, pejoratively, about the rich in India, it is often forgotten how they also gave much away. The system may now be derisory, condemned as paternalistic and arrogant. But it worked and laid the foundations for a more democratic and organised welfare state. Whether the one system is more successful than the other time alone will tell.

CHAPTER VII

Stately Pleasure Domes

"Les diamants chez nous sont innombrables,
Les perles dans nos mers incalculables.
C'est l'Inde, terre des merveilles."
"Chanson Hindou" (from a poem by Pushkin)

BETWEEN January and April, 1922, the Readings visited three Rajput states starting immediately after Christmas with Bikaner which lies in northern Rajputana, remote and strange, surrounded by golden deserts. In the fifteenth century a younger son of the House of Marwar (Jodhpur) called Beekar, set forth with 300 men-at-arms to carve out a kingdom for himself amid the sandhills. The barren country was inhabited by communities or cantons of Jats or Jits, as they were called in those days, tribes of Scythian origin who governed themselves in democratic fashion according to the ancient customs they had brought with them from Central Asia. The elders of the various cantons agreed to accept the overlordship of Beekar, as they knew they were unlikely to defeat him in battle and they needed protection from the depredations of whoever happened to be the Ruler of Delhi. The Jats were, and still are, largely agricultural people and they then had vast herds of cattle and sheep which throve on the scanty but in fact nourishing scrub vegetation of their desert tracts. Beekar therefore gained his desert kingdom without warfare and promised that he and his descendants would henceforth receive the *thika* of inauguration from the hands of the descendants of the elders of the principal Jat cantons. Rajput and Jat then joined together to conquer the rest of the desert area which eventually became the State of Bikaner. The spot selected by Beekar for his capital was the birthright of a Jat called Nera who surrendered it on condition that his name should be added to the Ruler's in perpetuity, hence Beekar-Nera, Bikaner.

So remote and savage was the countryside that it never became the prey of the Mahratta armies when they over-ran other parts of Rajasth'an. Beekar's descendants were astute politicians and allied themselves to the Moghul dynasty and Raja Rai Singh (who succeeded in 1573) was a brother-in-law of the great Emperor Akbar and one of his principal generals. Rai Singh's daughter married Akbar's son, the Emperor Jehangir.[1]

Sir Ganga Singh, Maharajah of Bikaner at the time of the Readings' visit, occupied a great position in Indian politics and social life. A man of striking personal beauty, charm and great ambition, he played a principal part in the founding of the Chamber of Princes and became its first Chancellor. During World War I he was much in London and France, his state having made great contribution to the war effort. He also took part in the peace negotiations at Versailles. A very cosmopolitan, a very sophisticated man, but one who never forgot his Rajput past. He was a wonderful host and did not ignore old friends even if they were quite unimportant people. Neither did he ever fail to keep contact with friends old and new who *were* very important people. Alice Reading writes on December 29th:

> I can't say much about our yesterday's arrival at Bikaner, must tell you more next week. The arrival gorgeous in the extreme. Two State carriages, four others with our suite. At the station the celebrated Bikaner Camel Corps . . . immovable as if carved out of grey granite. Then a huge crowd in every coloured turban. All the way along the route thousands of flags and on one side the Camel Corps for miles, on the other side the Nobles on thoroughbreds or Arabs, in every hue of brocade.

Bikaner camels are a breed apart. Colonel Tod said about them in 1823: "The camels, especially those used for expedition and the saddle, which bear a high price, are considered superior to any in India. They are beautifully formed, and the head possesses much blood and symmetry." They are elegantly pale in colour and their movements perfectly illustrate the term "ship of the desert".

Sir Ganga Singh's principal entertainment for his guests was the shooting of the Bikaner Imperial Sandgrouse, a bird found nowhere else in the world. Every British official in India, from Viceroy to District Officer, was expected to be a good shot. This derived from the ancient prerogative of royalty and aristocracy, the hunting of game for pleasure rather than the alleviation of hunger. Lord Reading had not been trained to field sports, but with his accustomed efficiency he set himself to practise with gun and rifle before ever he left England and he became perfectly adequate with both. It seems odd that to

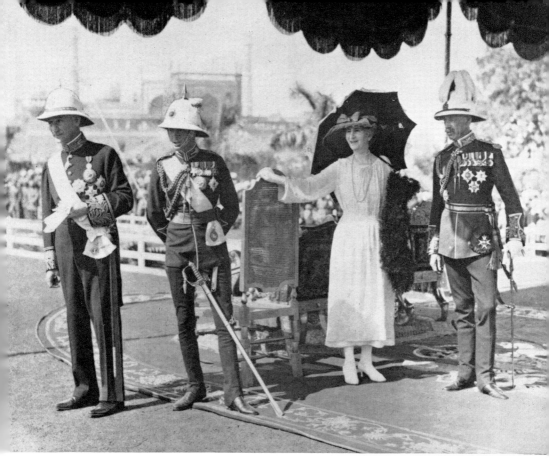

At the Durbar for H.R.H. the Prince of Wales in the Red Fort, Delhi, February 1922.
Left to right: H.E. the Viceroy, H.R.H. the Prince of Wales, H.E. Lady Reading,
H.E. General Lord Rawlinson of Trent, Commander-in-Chief

H.H. the Maharajah of Bikaner approaching the dais of the Diwan-i-Am in the
Red Fort during the Durbar

Their Excellencies in the courtyard of the Khailasa Cave, Ellora

govern India a man should be required to slaughter its fauna and bird-
life, particularly as at least two-thirds of India's population disapprove
of killing anything at all. The Maharajahs were certainly not among
that two-thirds and so it behoved a Viceroy to accept the magnificent
opportunities they offered him to bang away at fur and feather. Lord
Reading, like all of us who had the chance, greatly enjoyed his days
in jungles and on *jheels* (lakes for duck-shooting), and in the deserts
of Bikaner. Even if the quantities of what Alice Reading calls "mangled
feathers" might make some sensitive natures flinch, sport in India
took place in surroundings of such exquisite beauty, strangeness and
savagery that the experience could never be forgotten or repeated
anywhere else.

In order to shoot the Imperial Sandgrouse, the party assembled at
Gujner, a palace on the shores of a lake, largely artificially created,

> "Twice five miles of fertile ground
> With walls and towers were girdled round
> And there were gardens bright with sinuous rills."[2]

The windows, magic casements, opened on to water which lapped
soothingly all night in tranquillity, shattered first thing in the morning
by the opening fusillade of the duck-shoot, always the first event of the
sporting week. The butts stood on the other side of the lake and the
birds came in waves to drink, flying very similarly to Scotch grouse.
Guns were red hot before the flight finished and the birds were eaten
fresh every night after being plunged in boiling oil to remove skin as
well as feathers. Guests learnt at Bikaner what classic Indian cooking
should be as "Plat Bikaner" came round on vast trays. Each eager
Britisher would ask advice from an Indian neighbour before embarking
on the variety of bowls of delectable meat, fish and vegetables. Poor
Lady Reading's weak digestion prevented her from enjoying this very
real and very rare treat. She writes on magnificent vellum paper, headed
by a glowing crest:

Lallgarh. Bikaner. Jan. 2nd. I cannot refrain from using this gorgeous
paper, it may give you an insight into our surroundings. I tried to describe
our arrival and from that moment there has been a succession of thrills.
The Maharajah took us to the wonderful Fort so that I should see it by
daylight and examine the mosaics, lacquer and above all the jewels. Those
of the Maharajah of Benares are splinters in comparison. Such pearls and
emeralds, the latter in strings of about 6 chains together and then great

5

knobs of uncut emeralds and diamonds to keep them together. The most
beautiful tiaras and diadems and nearly all these have reverse side in
exquisite enamels mainly pinks and blues. I tried everything on and blazed
like a crystal chandelier in a white serge dress.

In the evening we drove to the Illuminations. All the Fort, in fact all
the Palaces are made of pinky red marble and everything, every turret,
every balcony, was outlined with pink, blue and mauve lights, absolute
fairyland with palms and tall trees in between.

We stopped in the courtyard where an enormous charcoal fire burnt in
centre and over this and through about 20 to 30 Fakirs clad in white
linen danced madly. It was a most thrilling sight for when they worked
themselves up with a religious frenzy they caught the red hot charcoal
and put it on their heads, stuck it in their mouths and played ball with the
glowing lumps. Afterwards some of our men went and looked at their
feet and they had not suffered at all (of course no shoes or stockings). If
they get blisters they have to undergo a penance for their sins.

Alice Reading calls all "holy men" in India *fakirs*, a very usual
mistake. The term is Mohammedan and would not apply in Bikaner.
She also describes:

> . . . a wizard who walked with bare feet on swords I could not touch, so
> sharp were their points. Altogether it was hopelessly uncanny, but won-
> derful and gorgeous. The Palace open to a dark blue velvet sky spangled
> with stars, then home to bed, home in a string of Rolls-Royce cars.
>
> Next day we went to the Jail. I have never seen anything so spick and
> span; all the inmates make carpets; we saw the whole process, dyeing,
> weaving, etc. and I ordered a huge one for Simla. In the afternoon a
> review of the Camel Corps, I think the most wonderful thing I have seen
> in India. Hundreds of camels and their riders, each camel with orange and
> red wool tassels hanging from crimson saddle bags, and round its neck
> *a dog collat of 3 large rows of white beads* like pearls!! Each driven by a red
> cord and its tail tied round to saddle. First they marched past in perfect
> line and then trotted, behind them a squadron of gorgeous cavalry on
> Arabs, a detachment of foot soldiers, so smart!
>
> *Gujner*, $\frac{3}{4}$ of an hour's drive, a splendid road through the dust to another
> fairy palace, only this time on an enchanted lake. From my bed I can see
> the sandgrouse rise over the lake and the wild duck. Early next morning
> they all sallied forth while I rested, and we then went down to a little
> landing stage to see the electric boats come in with immense bags of
> sandgrouse. In the afternoon we drove to a third palace, now in ruins,
> where we had tea. The whole Bikaner family goes there to say prayers, and
> the ghats are as sacred as at Benares.

Back in Bikaner I went to see the Maharanee; he took me himself alone to her, with his two boys and a little girl. A remarkable family picture. He, without a turban, in riding clothes, with the children on his knee and speaking perfect English. She in her eastern clothes, shut up in the Zenana, driving out in a motor with the shutters up, but watching us at every meal behind the stone screen pierced with holes inseparable from every eastern home.

Lalgarh is an enormous place, the zenana quarters beautifully open and airy on the second floor. The pierced stone screens surround every public room and it was sometimes a temptation to give a little wave to those unseen women watching and no doubt joking about all the guests who lounged or sported in the halls and colonnades. The holes in the stone were often occupied by basking pigeons and the sound of a pigeon's roulade on a hot still day always brings back Bikaner. A small boy in a crimson *pagri* wandered from court to court keeping the pigeons on the move.

One of the first duties of Lord Reading's Viceroyalty had been to decide the question of the heir to the *Gadi*[3] of Jaipur. The Rajputs of this state maintained an especial tradition of art and culture built up in conjunction with the Moghul dynasty whom they served with greater effect and consistency than any other of the four main clans of Rajasth'an. Jaipur lies closer to Delhi than any other state and has counted several rulers of unusual sophistication in its history. The custom of adoption has always been observed among Hindus, since it is religiously imperative to have a son to perform funeral rites. However, the English, in the days of the East India Company, regrettably took to annexing the states of rulers who died without legitimate male heirs. This practice ceased with the proclamation of 1858 in which Queen Victoria assumed the rulership of India from the Company, and special treaties between the states and the Crown came into being. The Crown disclaimed all desire for the extension of British territorial possessions in India "through encroachment on those of others". From that time onwards Hindu rulers were free to adopt an heir, provided their choice was approved by the Viceroy. Mohammedan rulers chose heirs according to Islamic Law. The visit to Jaipur in March, 1922, set the seal on an adoption arranged according to the old Maharajah's[4] personal choice:

March 22nd: a very thrilling week this, starting with the visit to Jaipur, which we did through the night as heat was so great. We arrived at 8.30

in the morning, were received informally by all the Court officials on a
lovely carpet, 300 years old, which I coveted! The heir, a boy of 11,[5] was
there to greet us. He has only just been made heir, H.E. settled the claim
in his favour to the everlasting gratitude of the Maharajah who is an old
man, paralysed in his legs. We had a marvellous reception all through the
streets and bazaars. The streets are lovely, the buildings all of Moorish
design in pinky stone picked out with white and such colour! Every few
yards a guard in brightest orange yellow with crimson turban. When we
reached the old Palace a crowd of nobles and a scarlet and gold Palanquin
awaited me where I had to lie at full length and be bumped and shaken
till we reached the Maharajah's private apartments. I was not going, but
he expressed a wish to see me so I was "swung" in on the Palanquin.

Imagine a very dirty gilded room, the walls covered with oleographs,
conspicuous among them a coloured one of the old Empress William,
Königen Louise. Big pieces of furniture swathed in dust sheets, dozens of
early Victorian gas chandeliers the colour of dust and only one beautiful
thing in the room, another priceless century-old carpet; and on it you
came upon — as if by chance — a figure seated cross-legged on the carpet,
no cushions, leaning against a bolster — the Maharajah!

A splendid man with magnificent head and straight features, olive-
skinned with a mane of grey hair and dark, flashing eyes. He looked every
inch a Rajput Chief, but a dying one. The heir sat drowsing cross-legged
as H.E. and the Maharajah had an interesting little talk (interpreted). The
boy was hung with emeralds and pearls and half-a-dozen little sons all
about the same age, with *kohl*-darkened eyes, stared at us as hard as they
could stare.

After 20 minutes or so we got up to go, but he asked us to remain another
5 minutes and then proceeded to present H.E. and me each with a lakh
of rupees for our favourite charity and to commemorate our visit to him
in the way we would like best. Wasn't it splendid of him? We parted and
were then taken to the Armoury and the Library. Wonderful weapons
from primæval age downwards, handles of gold, jade and precious stones.
The Library was glorious, volume after volume of priceless paintings
and missals from 11th to 16th century such as I shall never see again.

It is curious that Alice Reading should have received a Moorish
impression in the city of Jaipur. The Muslim cultural influence has
always been strong there; it was a refuge for Mohammedan artists
and craftsmen from time to time, as battles raged and Delhi rose and
fell. But the unique quality of the city is due to Rajah Sawai Jai Singh
(1699–1743), and the chief architect was a Hindu. Jai Singh stands out
as one of those giant figures found both in Europe and India in the

seventeenth and eighteenth centuries. Personalities inspired and gifted beyond the ordinary, who could turn their hand to the arts of war or peace impartially and who began to uncover the marvels of science. Jai Singh never visited Europe but studied the architectural plans of French and Italian cities and decided to build a new capital adjacent to the older fortress town of Amber.[6] He laid out his new city in broad arterial avenues, with intersecting streets. It can truly be said that Jaipur was the only planned city in India until Corbusier designed Chandigarh. Colonel Tod calls Jai Singh "the Machiavelli of his day" adding that he was "statesman, legislator and man of science" and that he "went deep" into the study of astronomy. He erected observatories, with instruments of his own invention, at Delhi, Jaipur, Ujjain, Benares and Mathura, and communicated with learned astronomers in Portugal, proving them incorrect in some of their calculations. His voluminous correspondence is contained in the Jaipur archive where no doubt there can also be found his translations into Sanskrit of Euclid's *Elements*, and Napier on logarithms. His reign coincided with the decline of Moghul power and the rise of the Mahrattas, with whom his predecessor, Jai Singh I., had made an alliance. Thus the exquisite new city and the remains of Amber, seat of his ancestors, have been preserved for the pleasure of twentieth-century tourists.

Lord Reading shot his first tiger at Jaipur. Lady Reading writes, March 22nd:

> A runner came in to tell me, "The Raj has shot a tigress". She was brought in later on the back of an elephant. I must say I wish I had been there instead I did my duty manfully, drove through the bazaars to please the people who gave me a wonderful reception, then visited booths put up in the grounds with arts and crafts of the country.

Next day the staff went pigsticking and black buck shooting while Lord Reading opened a new wing to the hospital, and finally:

> . . . at 5.30 after the sun had gone down came the "*clou*" of the stay, a visit to Amber. We drove several miles through picturesque villages and then came on these wonderful old ruins, a huge fortress perched on the top of a hill, with a winding road up. I was carried in a red and gold sedan chair arrangement, the rest rode on elephants all covered in scarlet and gold. It looked so wonderful – the procession up and up with these huge creatures. My chairmen in every colour of the rainbow. The fortress high, high up in the air, containing a lovely deserted palace all wonderfully preserved.

Six days later they were all at Alwar. "So far as we have observed it," writes Yvonne FitzRoy in her diary, "it is dusty and hot and peopled by amusing little hills that shoot untidy heads up from the plains." The Maharajah held strong views on how the princely order should be treated by the paramount power and he made up for any unimportance of his state by the magnetism of his personality. In addition to a brilliant intellect, he possessed sinister and mystical gifts which compelled attention even from those who could neither understand nor define them. At this early stage in the Reading Viceroyalty, Alwar was still determined to flatter and please. Later, when he had not got his way, he allowed natural malice to peep through the veneer of charming manners.

After an early arrival and an exhausting tour of the new palace before breakfast, the party swept out twenty-one miles to Seriska where they "beheld in the distance the white Palace that in Alwar adorns the humble name of shooting box". Lady Reading says that the tiger and leopard wall-paper in the rooms made her feel hotter than ever. The effect was similar to the tartan room at Balmoral.

After lunch we all sallied forth in motors, 4 or 5 miles, where we were met by elephants wonderfully painted. I had the Maharajah's own elephant, a highly-trained beast but still a *beast*. I hated it more than words can say but I would not give in, I had made up my mind to go to a tiger shoot on an elephant. After clambering on the creature's back I found a wonderful armchair awaiting me only arrived four days before from England. His Highness's own design, with pockets for camera, field-glasses, parasol, lens, refills, everything. We started—a dozen elephants in solemn procession in torrid heat. My gentleman on the elephant's head held a sunshade over me as well. We heaved, ambled and shook and rumbled along till we got to a tree where my nearly human elephant, at a word, broke off all the large branches so as not to impede my view of the guns who had advanced up the hill to where the beaters were driving down the tigers. I only waited to see two tigers come across the hill, then turned tail and departed. They say I was heard to murmur in descending, "a Rolls-Royce is good enough for me," and it's very likely. Still, I had achieved my object and went to rest, leaving the party another three hours' climb, which they followed up again the next day by an 8 hours' shoot.

Yvonne FitzRoy describes this shoot in detail and found it very dramatic. The purpose of a well-run tiger beat is to bring the quarry out to the guns as quietly and slowly as possible and with the least risk to the beaters. Yvonne describes rows of elephants, a band playing at intervals, bugles blowing, showers of stones thrown at a tiger at close range, which naturally emerged at full gallop, bounding and lashing its tail. It thus presented a desperately difficult shot and Lord Reading can be more than excused for "firing low". He probably missed it on purpose, realising he might wound it which would mean great danger for the beaters. This is a point which cannot have worried that particular Maharajah but, in his defence, it must be said that to bring tigers across six miles of mountainous country, through very sparse jungle, was a remarkable feat.

Yvonne describes a table under a spot-light outside the dining-hall at Seriska on which a baby goat was sometimes tethered, to be slain by a panther trained to this easy dinner in order to amuse guests. The goat did not appear for the Readings and Her Ex. enjoyed the state dinner, telling her host he was "a great Stage Manager". She adds in her letter:

> He really is a supremely interesting person; he dresses and plays the part. There is something intensely weird about him, and uncanny.

Yvonne confirms, saying that he was—

> . . . described not long ago, and by a rival Rajput, as the cleverest and bravest man in India (he killed a pig on foot with a knife the other day), a most perfect host, really thoughtful and considerate, but he remains a puzzle and a mystery. He is the centre of innumerable stories—many of them mythical no doubt but all significant. Stories indeed of amazing feats of courage but more often of hideous cruelty and, sometimes, darker inferences that remind one of tales of black magic and evil possession. You may think of him as Poet and Hero until—you catch the gleam of that wild animal smile or hear the goat wail once too often! The Jam Sahib [Ranji, of cricket fame] is a fellow guest and a more than welcome one—for the Jam is a dear through and through.

Her Ex. found a typed copy of the Maharajah's after-dinner speech laid by her plate to make sure she did not miss a word. It is characteristic of her that she saw this as a kindly act rather than an exhibition of vanity.

Yvonne's reflections on Gujner epitomise the dream quality of these gorgeous experiences, particularly now that the "Lion and the Lizard keep" so much of the glory of the princely state:

Gujner dreams of nothing, it is itself, the dreamer and the dream . . . By now I feel confident it has vanished. The lake has closed over that wonderful pink palace, compelled by some light-hearted and humorous magician, and all the Maharajah's preposterous furniture is lying derelict on the bank.

CHAPTER VIII

Crowded Hours

"Said Jesus, on whom be peace: 'The world is a bridge. Pass over it but build no house thereon. He who hopes for an hour hopes for eternity. The world is but an hour. Spend it in prayer. The rest is unseen.'"

> Inscription placed by Akbar the Great over the main gateway into Fatehpur Sikri.

BETWEEN the visit to Bikaner and those to Jaipur and Alwar, the whole of Viceregal Lodge prepared for the visit of the Prince of Wales. Lady Reading suffered continual sciatica and neuritis all through January and most of February:

Jan. 11th. Very little to relate this week owing to bad sciatica which I aggravated as I would get up. There was so much to plan and arrange. Amongst other things a servants' ball, planning the entertainments for the Prince, inspection of tents for the visitors . . . Tomorrow Lord Northcliffe arrives and ought to be interesting on his travels. Besides he will be able to tell us some of the inner workings of things. In spite of many correspondents one misses news red hot from Downing Street. To our great relief the Prince is having wonderful receptions everywhere . . . We are letting him off very lightly here in the way of ceremonies. Only one state dinner, one large ball, then one gay fancy dress dance, and a dinner and dance here of young people with a jazz band. A Durbar at the wonderful Fort in the afternoon where all the Princes come in their best, a garden party follows and ends up with illuminations of the Fort and gardens. Then polo galore and a dinner given by the Princes.

H.E. is working from early morning till night. Yesterday an Indian wrote me that the Bishop of Calcutta said that his father's birthday wish to one of his sons was, "May you have a year full of difficulties," and my Indian friend added: "I expect that the Gods began paying that kind of compliment to His Ex. the day you both sailed for India. I can hear them saying (and do you think they nudge each other as they speak?), 'We shall not get this kind again. Let us pile on the difficulties'." This Indian is a great friend of mine, the first woman Indian Barrister, she is now going home to be called at the Middle Temple, is one of the cleverest women out here and has her finger on the pulse of many things and has been a true friend and adviser to me in many ways.

Lady Reading is referring to Cornelia Sorabji, a Parsee who was all she describes.[1] Parsees are a distinct community of Persian origin, Zoroastrians by religion, centred largely in Bombay but found in industry and the professions all over India. They were sometimes accused by nationalists of being over-fond of the British but they have had hotheads from time to time in the nationalist ranks. Being highly educated and free of taboos which frustrated Hindu and Muslim society, they took a reasonable view of what the British were trying to do. They were mostly people of property and therefore tended to appreciate law and order.

On January 25th, Alice Reading reports that she had not been beyond the four walls of her bedroom for a week but she had been well enough to admire presents from—

... the Ruler of Nepal[2] who sent an offering to H.E. consisting of, amongst other things, two tiny little ponies. They came to the front door, 2 elephants, male and female, came only as far as the Border. A large tray full of gold coins, some as small as this O. A magnificent tiger skin and about a dozen musk rats' bags, brought to my door but promptly ejected because of stench. Rolls of brocade, switches to keep flies off, all sorts of barbaric offerings. All these are valued and we can keep what we want by paying into Treasury their value, but this is not much fun! Events are moving fast and on the 31st we are promised Civil Disobedience by Gandhi, which means non-payment of taxes, shutting up shops and general unpleasantness. So far (imberufen) H.E. has been more than justified by his allowing the Prince to come. I am afraid it has been a hard time for him, poor boy, but hope he will enjoy Delhi.

It is clear to us now that the Prince came too late to India, but he came to no harm and says himself[3] that he left without any realisation of imminent change. He reported to Edwin Montagu on his return that he did not think India any longer a place for a white man to live in, but only a small proportion of far-seeing civilians would have agreed with him in 1921, and no-one in the Army. Everyone in India enjoys a tamasha, a spectacle, so quite sizeable crowds turned out to look at him. Naturally the Princes welcomed one of their own order and the British were cheered and encouraged by his presence.

31st January. Still convalescing, but have been promoted to little walks. To-day revisited the Prince's house to see what mistakes had been made in my absence. I asked them to have some suitable pictures sent from Simla as walls looked so bare and found they had promptly despatched some fly-blown hunting scenes from the A.D.C.s' passage to adorn my schemes of grey-green and gold, so it is a good thing I am about again to counteract their taste . . .

To-day the Civil Disobedience was to have started, but visitors to the town report everything very cheerful. It is a terrible thing for the shop-keepers when *hartal* is announced as it means they must close, otherwise are boycotted and may have their windows smashed.

We are besieged by people wanting invitations, some funny, mostly impudent. One elderly female wrote last week she wished her name put down for a *car* during the Prince's visit as otherwise it would be difficult for her to attend *all* the functions. Another wrote we should be pleased to hear she had arrived with her daughter and all invitations for Balls, dinners, etc. were to be sent to a certain address! The Invitation A.D.C. is getting old and haggard.

As time drew nearer for the royal arrival, Lady Reading's health slowly improved and it is interesting to note her placid attitude to the possibility of political unrest. Her refusal to be ruffled must have helped the Viceroy, who carried a very heavy burden of responsibility. It is easy to mock at the complacency of the British at this time, but steady nerves are not to be despised and must count as an essential attribute of leadership.

On February 8th she notes:

All our preparations are complete for the Prince's arrival, now we have only to await developments of the political situation. Everyone here is very cheerful; I should like the pessimists at home to look on here at times. Not that the situation is without gravity but Gandhi has now exposed his hand and the newspapers (with one exception, an ultra-extremist organ) are on the side of the Government and praise H.E.'s patience and condemn Gandhi's tactics. It remains to be seen what attitude they take up in Delhi. The Gandhi Cap is seen about a great deal. I wish it were possible for a Viceroy to go down amongst the people and talk to them and nail the lies to the counter. But apart from the language, this is impossible.

The tents are lovely, a huge sitting room with bedroom, bathroom adjoining, running water, electric light, big writing tables, wardrobes, anything so unlike a tent cannot be imagined, but they are very hot in the middle of the day.

At present the Cabinet is sitting in Council Chamber with locked doors after partaking of a very good tea in my drawing-room. I have had great fun with them as the Board of Works Minister had the Fort at the top of our Park here painted with red ochre instead of leaving it old brick. I insisted it should be re-done and waited for the Cabinet to come out, and particularly the Finance Minister, and told them they must re-paint it. There are some Indians on the Council, particular friends of mine. Must stop this rambling epistle, as news has just reached me to come to bungalow at once as the Superintendent is hanging pictures. As his taste runs to "Kiss Mummy good-night" style in broad gold frames, it is time I intervened.

On February 16th, Lady Reading writes a first instalment on the Prince's visit, in a wobbly hand, obviously exhausted but, as she says, "not one single discordant note, *thank heaven*". As a matter of fact there were many discordant notes if contemporary accounts are to be believed, but there was no violence after the initial rioting on the day of the Prince's arrival in Bombay.

Lady Reading is speaking as a person about people and in this way her records have value:

> After tea H.E. and I walked over to Prince's bungalow with him. He was delighted with all the arrangements and most appreciative of everything in the house. We dined a house-party of 60 and young people came in the evening and danced to our new Jazz Band.

At the State Banquet she notes that when the Prince responded to the toast to his health he was—

> . . . intensely nervous; what with his tight red tunic and collar and his speech (tho' he only read it) he was very glad when it was over.

At the Durbar in the Fort she—

> . . . would have felt happier if I had not sat on a gold throne chair with scarlet velvet cushions embroidered in gold, in a petunia satin dress, but I hope I looked like a fuchsia. The Prince was much too worried by his tight red tunic and speech to notice. The Princes looked wonderful, some had fringes of cabochon emeralds all round their turbans.

She notes that the Prince was "in radiant spirits when he had not to make a speech" and that he shared her minced chicken and rusks and was "very jolly". He came to see her every day and told her that the carefully prepared bungalow was the first "home" he had had since England.

At one point in the visit he went out to see the beginnings of New Delhi and met Sir Edwin Lutyens[4] and Mr. Baker,[5] the rival architects:

> The Prince looked at everything and insisted on going to the stone yard where hundreds of Indian workmen and their families gave him a rousing send-off and even cheered, remarkable for an Indian crowd.

Like Alice Reading, the Prince of Wales succeeded in personal contacts —

> On Monday we all went to the Polo. H.R.H., H.E. and I sat on a cretonne covered sofa; the 2 jumped so for joy at every good shot that I bumped up and down and I am sure springs were ruined.

This was a famous game in polo annals at which the Jodhpur team beat Patiala, who had been the winners of this tournament for a number of years. The Jodhpur team were under the eye of Sir Pertab Singh,[6] the Bayard of India, a character so famous at that time and the years before that a digression must be made to explain him.

He was of the family of Idar from which the heir to the Jodhpur *gadi* has to be chosen if there is no direct heir of the body. Friend of Queen Victoria and a Rajput of the Rajputs, always to the fore in times of battle, a courteous host, faithful friend at all times. Sir Henry Newbolt wrote a poem about how Sir Pertab Singh lost caste and had to do penance because he carried to burial the body of a young Englishman, son of a dear friend, who died at Jodhpur. Sir Pertab felt that he was in a father's place to this boy who died so far from home. It was said that if the youth of Jodhpur (many of whom fought for us in both wars) returned from battle uninjured, Sir Pertab would ask: "Why are you not dead?" Yvonne FitzRoy describes him at this famous game:

> Sir Pertab himself sat in the enclosure watching the game which, at first, went badly against a team of which his favourite son[7] was the leading spirit. He sat rigid; only as the score mounted against his team 2-1, 3-1, 4-1, his hands twitched and his eyes were not quite steady. At five-all he smiled for the first time and when "time" went at a score of 6-5 he was totally hidden by a surging crowd led by H.R.H. cheering him to the echo.

Polo had to take the place of "battles long ago" between Prince and Prince. Moreover, the Patiala team were Sikhs, great people, but not Rajputs and therefore defeat by them would seem to Sir Pertab all the more of a tragedy.

At the State Ball they danced the State Lancers, a "must" in Vice-regal circles in those days:

> The Prince knew nothing of them, Mrs. Ronnie Greville still less. We were all breathless with laughter and so were the onlookers and it was voted the merriest State Ball Viceregal Lodge had ever seen.
>
> The last day a People's Fair on the Maidan, people all uninvited, between 15 and 20,000 elbowing and pushing and swarming round the Prince who was on horseback. I only went to receive him and then escaped as heat and crowds so terrific no sports could take place. Altogether just what we wanted — a People's entertainment and practically three-quarters of them Indians.

This episode must have given headaches to those in charge of security. The Prince insisted on doing much the same at Lahore. The British certainly did not walk in fear and trembling in those days, as is so often now implied.

It is hardly surprising to find Her Ex. taking to her bed after this overwhelming week, but she "crawled out" to meet:

> . . . a Maharajah[8] whom I had my eye on for some time, who was so enamoured (not of me) but of my scheme for building the hospital that he then and there offered me the money, all I needed without further begging, that is about 5 lakhs or £30,000. On top of Prince's visit this was almost too much for me. He called in his Prime Minister and told me to tell him what I wanted and alone, the three of us, we settled it there and then. I only wanted the Hospital and, as a reward for my restraint, this night an American staying here and his wife promptly offered me £3,000 for instruments and equipment. Isn't it wonderful of them all? I had collected £25,000,[9] now that will go to the Hardinge College so I have done all I wanted in the first year. Hurrah!

A plan to rest and "go to bed early" had to be cancelled because of visits from the Governors of Madras and Bombay who asked if they could come and discuss their problems with the Viceroy in person. They both brought full staffs so the princely tents came in useful:

> We were a very cheery party, about 20 young men each one nicer than the other and I have 5 girls still staying here besides two married women so I could leave them to their own devices. H.E. and the Governors had so much to discuss and talk over that they were busy all the time. But we took them to the new Delhi. I am anxiously watching its progress. Mr. Baker, who is answerable for the Secretariat, says 4 years will see it done

whereas Sir Edwin Lutyens says 7 years for the Palace IF the money is forthcoming! It is the greatest thing of its kind I have ever seen and makes one's brain whirl, so overpowering. What the inside will cost I am afraid to think, as the interior of the vast marble halls and reception rooms, etc., are all supposed to be covered with mosaic and inlay and coloured marbles. The Viceroy has three studies. I courteously refrained from asking Sir Edwin if he was supposed to keep his papers in all three! But I thought a lot! I have promised to help in a scheme to lay out the gardens as everyone loves my garden here, it really is wonderful, since November we have had every room full of flowers.

From contemplation of an Imperial City yet to be, the Readings went off to Agra to see the buildings of an Imperial City that once was. Lord Reading's enjoyment of the visit must have been greatly marred by hearing of the resignation, in unhappy circumstances, of his friend and colleague Edwin Montagu, Secretary of State for India. He could not have lasted, anyway, under a Conservative government, but it was ironic that he should be deliberately forced out of office by the Liberal who had appointed him, Lloyd George. The circumstances concerned a telegram from the Viceroy referring to the British negotiations with Turkey in connection with the Treaty of Sèvres and the effect of these on Muslim feeling in India. Mr. Montagu carelessly published this telegram without consulting his Cabinet colleagues and the Prime Minister demanded his resignation. Lord Reading felt he might have to resign too, in loyalty to his colleague, but he was in no way implicated and was persuaded that to leave his work in India just as he had started would be dangerous policy. All this lay heavy on his heart and mind as he gazed upon the deserted glories of the Moghul Emperors. At the same time it was decided to arrest Gandhi, whose policy of passive resistance had developed into acts of open sedition. Lord Reading made this arrest reluctantly and to this day right-wing opinion criticises him for procrastination as did the Civil Service in India at the time. Their primary responsibility was law and order and long-term policies of gradual education for freedom did not appeal to harassed District Officers and Police Superintendents. In one of his last letters to Reading, Edwin Montagu writes:

... the fact of the matter is, Rufus, that people here are fed up with India, and it is all I can do to keep my colleagues steady on the accepted policy, let alone new instalments of it.[10]

Gandhi was arrested on March 10th and on March 12th the Readings went to Agra for the week-end:

> March 14th. Rather a crowded week of events as just as we were starting for Agra news of Montagu's resignation reached us. This disturbed, but did not spoil our outing. It is so useless to talk of things political when a letter takes three weeks to reach you. He, Montagu, was immensely liked by the vast majority of Indians and general regret is expressed at his departure.

Alice Reading is extremely discreet about this, as about Gandhi's arrest, but even allowing for discretion, it seems clear that the Taj proved adequate compensation for the bad news. She says, as many others have done:

> It was full moon and I shall never forget it, I had the greatest trouble to keep from crying it was so beautiful, so peaceful and so sad. You arrived at the great sandstone arched gateway and when inside you looked straight from the obscurity of the small quadrangle, only lighted by a flickering lamp, to the long walk of stone flanked by cypresses, and reflected in the water lay the entire building with four towers carved in snow white marble, like pierced ivory. The only glimmer of light the little centre dome where the tombs of Shah Jehan and his favourite wife lie, in alabaster inlaid with jewels.

The Taj has been dreadfully vulgarised in reproduction, but to see it in reality is an emotional experience, not because of the romance attached to it but because it is of absolutely perfect proportions. Yvonne FitzRoy found it "infinitely remote" and felt that it gained by freedom from personality. That is the secret of Muslim art and architecture, since the representation of persons is forbidden in the Koran for fear of idol worship. This too may have touched Alice Reading in the unconscious depths of her being—"Thou shalt not make unto thyself any graven image, nor the likeness of anything that is in heaven above or the earth beneath." The Viceregal party were accompanied by the Commissioner of Agra and the Surveyor of Archaeology, and it is surprising to find that, though both "very charming men", they were "singularly deficient in any knowledge of the monuments and places". This was a thousand pities, for Agra is as full of history as Delhi, and the "two charming men" can never have had an audience more anxious to learn. "The Fort was remarkable," goes on Her Ex. —

. . . and the old town of Fatehpur Sikri in a marvellous state of preservation with another Pearl Mosque so beautiful that I was almost faithless to my first love, the Pearl Mosque at Delhi. We were met by the Priests and after H.E. and I had accepted some biscuits which subsequently found their resting place in the Aide's pocket, we had our shoes covered and entered the Mosque. H.E.'s and my coverings were of electric blue velvet embroidered in gold, the others had plain white felt.

She always notices these details, evidence of the instinctive Indian awareness of hierarchical ritual. The full story of Akbar's dead city of Fatehpur-Sikri seems to have passed her by. There cannot have been time to tell her, unless the archaeologist really did not know and did not try. The Emperor Akbar[11] built the city as a thank-offering for the birth of his son (later Jehangir) and a wonderful place it is. There he gathered together sages and teachers of all faiths, and would sit for hours listening to their disputations, from which he evolved his dream of a universal faith—Din Ilāhi—which would make all men one. Here his Rajput wife had her apartments, and his Christian wife as well. Legend has it that the water supply failed and the Great Moghul and all his train moved back to Delhi. In those days there was a wonderful road between Agra and Fatehpur-Sikri, lined on either side by prosperous shops and houses. Now these have all gone and in the Readings' time there was nothing but dust, small mud villages and the shacks of wandering gypsies.

6

CHAPTER IX

The Second Round

"The night air smelt very good . . . and the crescent of Islam rode in a
clear sky . . . From my bed I could see the Squadron, and beyond it the
jagged hills of Afghanistan, with Orion's belt above them. I used to
struggle hard to keep awake to enjoy the world a little longer."

Bengal Lancer by Francis Yeats-Brown

BEFORE returning to Simla in the spring of 1922, the Readings
went on a Frontier tour. A new appraisal of frontier problems
awaited the Viceroy. The Treaty signed in November, 1921,
contained the refusal of the British to vacate tribal areas of the North-
West Frontier though the Afghans disputed this clause. The Frontier
was held for Britain at a vast cost to the Indian Treasury (six crores of
rupees—£4,500,000) and Lord Reading wished to come to some agreement with the military authorities and, above all, with the home
government, as to how this sum could be reduced. Lord Rawlinson,[1]
the Commander-in-Chief, headed a Committee to consider the whole
question and he and leading members of his staff met Lord Reading at
Peshawar in March. Alice Reading wrote one letter on this two-day
trip:

> April 3rd. Here we are, right on the Frontier, and it is the first place
> strange to say that has reminded me of England since I landed in India.
> Such green grass and tall trees, bushes of roses and most attractive houses
> with tiled roofs instead of the usual Indian flat roof. Then it actually
> rained, two showers, and we all went out to see and feel and rejoice at it.
> The garden here is heavenly with rows of orange trees in full bloom, beds
> of pansies and a rose-garden with such Maréchal Niel! There is plenty of
> water and a splendid system of irrigation and no monsoon such as we
> suffer from in Simla and Delhi.

Yvonne FitzRoy underlines the contrasts in scenery. She went with an
escort to Shabkadr where:

> . . . we had tea with the two English officers who control this outpost with
> the assistance of the Mohmand Militia, a levy of the local tribe, and

climbed to the highest tower to survey the country. A mile away ran the line of barbed wire and watchtowers that for fifteen miles guard the boundary of British territory, beyond them in an immense horseshoe the mountains of the Frontier Tribes, arid, desolate and extraordinarily beautiful. The plain with its fat cattle and fatter crops and the green and silver of its fields and rivers stretches away from their feet to a remote distance. What wonder it has been a debateable land of promise throughout every page of its history.

Her Ex. takes up the tale:

H.E. and the Commander-in-Chief and a dozen Generals have been to the Afghanistan frontier, they took an armoured car along and we drive with an orderly on the box with a gun cocked. They are a rough lot up here and shoot (as a man in hospital explained to me) like we use a handkerchief. Such a splendid race of men, very tall, as lithe as panthers, swarthy hair bobbed as the girls do at home, also locks plastered on their cheeks. They shoot members of their own family or anyone who happens to offend them or whose grandfather or great-grandfather offended them. One said yesterday (interpreted): "I shot him, I bore him a grudge but I don't know for what, it was a family grudge."

The hospitals here are crowded with men and even women and children with gun-shot wounds in face, legs and arms, all from the same causes. I have spent my time while H.E. has been away going from hospital to hospital listening to grievances and trying to help. Have already visited one Zenana Purdah Women's Hospital, 1 large Civil Hospital, 1 enormous Mission Hospital, 1 Military Indian and 1 Military European besides an Officers' Wives Home, so it is not all play.

At the Mission Hospital they have an enormous courtyard with beds all round open to the sky. The caravaners come in and are attended to there in rows. One woman had her nose cut off because she was unfaithful! Squatting all over the floor are the relations all rolled up in old blankets, shawls, carpets and sacks. The marvel is that anyone recovers from an operation, but they all do, the air is so pure and so lovely they don't seem to need water. The caravans come in just by the garden gate. All the camels huge and shaggy with their saddle bags full of stuff to exchange and barter. Mules, with their owners astride, their bundles belching every colour of the rainbow. H.E. had a wonderful trip, at every stopping place a goat and fruit, etc. offered him. Am thankful to say that goat returned else I should have a herd by now.

April 4th. To-day I was to have gone to the Khyber Pass, but they have all gone without me as have been very seedy and had to stay in bed. We leave to-morrow for Dehra Dun if I am alright, which I shall be. If possible, shall drive to the Pass in the morning, or half way. Last night a dinner party, I could not attend. People came from miles away each with a revolver, men and women! How is that for you who sleep in peace at home, or even for us further away? Some of these women are real heroines doing their work silently, bravely, knowing each time their husband goes out he may never return alive. Here in Hospital is a pretty young Matron whose husband was Doctor there. One night he was called down by a man, shot dead, as 5 years before he had failed to cure his (the man's) son. This woman came back to the Hospital where her husband was murdered to work amongst his enemies and to devote her life to these people who had taken *his* life and this is only one example amongst many.

Alice Reading is telling the story of Mrs. Starr, who reappears in these letters as the heroine of a frontier incident.

Frontier service was hard on women, since there were stations, like Razmak, where wives and children were not allowed. In those days the Government did not take much interest in the family life of its servants. No provision was made for ferrying about service men's dependents, of any rank. A posting to Razmak might be for two years, with short infrequent leaves; everyone took it as a matter of course.

The time now came to move back again to Simla via Dehra Dun and a brief stop at Taxila where Sir John Marshall[2] was busy uncovering Graeco-Buddhist remains, relics of the days when the remote ancestors of the Rajput Princes first came down from the north. Her Ex.'s carriage on the train filled with roses at every stop and she writes from Dehra Dun:

> It certainly is a thrilling life if you are well and able to get about a lot. I must say, not seeing the Khyber Pass was a disappointment. The tragedy was I visited five hospitals because I thought I would get my work over first, then enjoy myself and that was the result. H.E. had a wonderful time, walking and riding, climbing and motoring and visiting all sorts of strange tribes and peoples. I sent the maids and Smith [H.E.'s valet] too and Smith on his return informed me he "had made a mental note to re-adjust his previous conception of a caravan, as up till then he had always thought it went on wheels."

It was Smith who told Sir Harcourt Butler that the Terai, the huge grassy plain at the foot of the Nepalese Himalaya, reminded him of Norfolk.

> Simla. 8,000 feet up! April 18th. Such a changed Viceregal Lodge! I hope future Vicereines will be grateful to me for changing (in my sitting room)

white enamel paint and green billiard table cloth walls to a most lovely waxed walnut room panelled to the ceiling.

Sir Harcourt Butler says in one letter home: "Viceroys enrich the language about each other." He could have added with truth: "and Viceroys' wives about each other's interior decoration." Lady Reading vastly improved the house in Simla, not least by the introduction of a number of good pictures and chandeliers from Calcutta which made a suitable background for a visit from the new Governor of Bengal, Lord Lytton,[3] with his staff.

"Every day in every way I get better and better," is the opening of Alice Reading's next letter:

You will see "Coué"[4] has reached us here and I am trying hard to persuade myself into being well. It would be such a comfort if more people took it up, as it is such an aid to conversation and fills in many blanks. Take one evening alone when perhaps 20 strange women and 20 strange men are brought up to me, each for five minutes. I should be spared racking my brains for suitable subjects for conversation.

We are having a car up here for the first time, having only used horses up till now. The roads are very narrow and everyone walks on them. You see a coolie coming along with a wardrobe on his head, ayahs pushing prams, natives selling betel nut by the roadside and over it all, clouds of white dust. For this reason I need a closed car as driving in a victoria is a penance. But I tremble for the passers-by.

I must tell you the following story of our head coachman who has been here many years. I complained that one of our carriage horses sneezed all the time, which was most disagreeable. In the afternoon he said to the Aide: "I am sorry Her Ex. had to complain about the horse. I had noticed its sneezing but thought it was rather refreshing!!"

This story went round Simla a year later and it is delightful to find such stories in Alice Reading's letters. There were a number of standard ones, some of which have been repeated by biographers. She tells all of them herself with amusement at her own expense. She saw, heard and understood a good deal more than the rather simple people around her realised. She notes that whenever she has a bright idea for a party or for improvements in the house and garden, her Staff tell her that "it has never been done". This, she says, "goads me to frenzy".

She finds the hills wonderful, rhododendron trees in bloom as big as oaks, and daffodils at Mashobra where the tumbledown state of "The Retreat" is a relief after so many palaces. She hears of a Russian woman who has been on a trip to the hills with "15 odd natives" and who can tell fortunes, is a theosophist and a believer in the occult—

> . . . It sounds something to divert the monotony of entertaining big-wigs; I shall be on her track.

This lady turned out a disappointment and was last seen by Her Ex. taking a Bank at vingt-et-un with the Aides and "scooping in annas".

> May 11th. This morning a searching examination of a large house on the estate H.E. gave me to do what I like with and I have promptly equipped it and offered it to European nurses, 8 at a time, for a rest home in the hills. Many of these nurses work years in the plains, too poor to take the journey or get much needed fresh air. One of them has been 11 years in Delhi through all the scorching summers, never had a holiday and mostly alone in a hospital of 200 patients with only ward men to help, besides the doctors' daily visits; what a life! On the whole people develop an intense love for this country as lots of men, soldiers, civil servants, etc., after a long life of service here cannot bear the idea of never coming back to India. The men wear much better than the women. A great many Europeans who have been out here 35 years are hale and hearty, riding and shooting at 60 to 70; whereas the quite young women look faded and seem to lose energy. Some of them have a lovely time. Simla is a hotbed of flirtations and more, where every Jack has someone else's Jill!

Sir Harcourt Butler reports about this time:

> Some of the women in Simla object to the Readings going to church. One might have thought this a compliment rather than a form of self-indulgence. It only shows how much unoccupied time there must be in Simla.

There was no unoccupied time for Alice Reading. Her letters and Yvonne's diary tell of constant visits to the proposed site of the new hospital, committee meetings and the inevitable round of balls, dinners, levées and small intimate parties at which she introduced music and card-games as a variation of setting to partners all round the room. The political situation appeared calmer but the Viceroy had to unravel a number of tangles in internal administration. Financial difficulties loomed large and the provinces were incensed by what was known as "The Meston award"[5] which fixed the contribution of the provinces to the centre too high for the liking of the former. It was decided to send out Lord Inchcape,[6] chairman of the P. & O. Steamship Co., heading a committee to wield the axe and see what could be done to balance the

Indian budget. All through the first part of 1922 the Viceroy was engaged in clearing the ground for this committee and its subsequent success owed much to his preparations. Uncertainty about the future disturbed recruitment in England for the Civil Service and a confidential document suggesting a stepping-up of Indian recruitment got into the press causing the P.M., Lloyd George, to make a speech emphasising that recent reforms in India were only an experiment. This upset the Indians so the Viceroy had his hands full keeping the peace. Lady Reading's gifts were particularly important in such a disturbed atmosphere when British, as well as Indians, were poised to take offence whatever the Viceroy and his government might do. The fact that she herself did not find time or inclination to study administrative and political subjects prevented her from developing partisan opinions. Everyone who came into her house was her guest, each to be made as happy and comfortable as possible. To this end she bent all her energies and taxed her fragile health.

On May 18th she describes a farewell dinner to Mr. Srinivasa Sastri,[7] a distinguished politician of the middle way who was about to depart for a tour of Canada, Australia and New Zealand with the purpose of enquiring into the condition of Indians living in those countries. This was part of Lord Reading's policy of supporting Indians in the Dominions and Crown Colonies, with especial reference to South Africa and Kenya. "As a Liberal and a Jew, he hated any form of discrimination."[8] Sastri did not have to deal with Africa and his reception and success in the three Dominions proved to be a credit to him and to them.

> The Sastri dinner took place very successfully. All the rank and fashion of Simla, an excellent dinner and good music. Sastri took me in to dinner, he is very interesting but it is difficult to make him talk. H.E. proposed his health and gave a death blow to murmurs and fault-finding against him in the press. He replied — at first disappointing but as he warmed to it, very good indeed, but 40 minutes rather long for an after-dinner speech. Excellent matter, a musical voice and a marvellous command of the language. A quiet week-end at Mashobra, most of the party spent part of the time in the orchard where the black cherries and apricots are ripe. The roads looked so picturesque with crowds of girls and men all in their best, going to the yearly Fair and Marriage Mart.

Hillwomen do not observe purdah and are, when young, startlingly beautiful. Smith, valet, also went to the Fair as a spectator, all by himself, and was much teased for returning all by himself. To which he replied that he was "no judge of girls".

A character who appears very frequently in Lady Reading's letters and in Miss FitzRoy's diary is the Maharajah of Patiala.[9] The galloping hooves of polo ponies played an unceasing *obbligato* in the background of Indian life and both the Viceroy's staff team, and the Bodyguard team contested every tournament hotly and often successfully. The Maharajah of Patiala, being much at home socially in Simla, always had a couple of teams handy for tournaments.

Patiala is a Sikh state. The Sikhs were a sect that broke away from Hinduism in the sixteenth century under the influence of their first *guru* or teacher, Nanak. He taught an ethic very similar to the Sermon on the Mount and stressed the unity of God, the futility of ritual worship and the unreality of caste. These moves towards a universal brotherhood of man were in the air in India at that time, as we have seen with the Emperor Akbar. It was Akbar who granted the site of the Golden Temple at Amritsar, the centre of Sikhism, to the fourth *guru* in line from Nanak, in 1577. Jehangir attacked the Sikhs, not because of their religion but because they took sides against him in a rebellion. The fifth *guru*, Arjun, under whose leadership the *Adi Granth*, the holy book of the Sikhs, came into being, was tortured and executed by Jehangir in 1606. From then onwards the Sikhs withstood Islam with all their strength and changed from a peaceful mystic sect to a brotherhood of warriors. Under Aurangzeb[10] they met with religious as well as political oppression and the story goes that when the ninth *guru*, Tegh Bahadur, lay in prison in Delhi, he was accused of peering towards the apartments of the Emperor's ladies, to which he replied: "Emperor Aurangzeb, I was on the top story of my prison, but I was not looking at thy private apartments or at thy Queens. I was looking in the direction of the Europeans who are coming from beyond the seas to tear down thy Purdahs [curtains] and destroy thy Empire."

Under the tenth (and last) *guru*, Govind Singh (1675–1708), Sikh military power became seriously organised and the brotherhood bound together by two sacraments, not unlike those of the Christian church. Baptism consisted of drinking water consecrated by the stirring of a dagger, and communion of partaking, all together, of a consecrated *chupattee* passed from hand to hand, thus effectively breaking caste rules. The fraternity took the name of *Khalsa*, meaning "Pure". It was *Guru* Govind who insisted on the rules for long hair and unshaven beards and complete abstention from tobacco. In addition he ordered the wearing of a ceremonial dagger, *kirpan*, a steel bangle round the wrist and short pants rather than the long and full trousers of the northern Punjaubi Mussulman or the *dhoti* of the Hindu. Like most religious rules these were of practical use but became symbolic and hold fast to this day. There is no more closely-bound community than the Sikhs and, owing to their freedom from dietary taboos, caste and purdah, they are magnificent people physically and will go anywhere and do anything. They resemble in some ways the Orders of Chivalry of the Middle Ages; they are religious warriors and no regiments in the Indian Army have a finer record than the Sikh regiments. They fought in both world wars and, what is not usually known, stood by the British to a man in the Mutiny. Without the Sikhs there would have been no re-taking of Delhi, which was the turning point in that tragic episode.

But before the Sikhs threw in their lot with the British they fought against us hard and bitterly, falling into some errors of judgment after the decline and death of their temporal leader, Rajah Ranjit Singh, who maintained reasonably friendly relations with the British for most of his life. At the end of the second Sikh War (Chilianwala, 1846) the British took over the ravaged Punjaub and made it into a model for all India and this province came to the rescue of the rest in 1858. The Sikh states — Patiala, Nabha, Kapurthala and Jhind — were carved out of Punjaubi territory (some of it in the Simla hills) after the break-up of the Sikh kingdom.

Patiala's appetite and dazzling appearance fascinated the Viceregal staff. He stood over six-feet tall, weighed twenty stone and dressed magnificently in a mixture of European and Indian style. He had the fine beard and hair of his race, neatly combed and netted. He played a good game of tennis and also cricket in spite of his size, and would have been a better polo player if he could have brought himself to go on a diet. His ponies (*sic*: they were horses) were magnificent heavy-weights, as indeed they needed to be. He was great fun, thoroughly enjoyed a party and everything that went with it. In later life his uncontrolled appetites destroyed him but at this time he was a welcome character in Simla life. His team, known as "The Tigers", played in black and orange striped singlets, looking more like vast wasps than jungle cats.

In June, the Readings attended the wedding of General Delamain's[11] daughter, Honor. The Viceroy lent the State carriage for the bride and the flowers were all arranged from the Viceregal gardens. This was the usual custom in Simla where florists did not exist and the alternative to the State carriage would be a rickshaw with the bridegroom on horseback. Her Ex. notes that Patiala looked magnificent at the wedding in Staff Officer's uniform "with huge pearl and diamond earrings. This disturbed my devotions considerably."

In late June, Air Marshall Sir John Salmond[12] came to stay, on his way to the Frontier where he was to inspect the possibilities of air power to take the place of a large field force:

> All the airmen here I have spoken to seem most optimistic on the chances of flying to India. This time they do not claim to do it in 3 days as Commander Binney does in England. Fancy if I could come over on a weekend visit to you all!!
>
> My hospital is going on slowly as regards plans, but money for it coming in well, the chief consideration. I have collected myself about £50,000, this is without the large sum promised by the Raja [of Nabha]. I am taking him this week to see the site, he sent me word if there was any other place I preferred I was to have it, it is well to be a Maharajah!

In August the Erleighs arrived but the principal festivities arranged for them, including the first Fancy Dress dance to be held in Viceregal Lodge for years, had to be postponed because of Court mourning for the Duchess of Albany. Her Ex. is sad about having to abandon her prettiest dresses for an "old black velvet". Dame Nellie Melba[13] came to stay and "looms large on the horizon, she is a very pleasant guest. Loves young men, bridge and being made a fuss of, so she is in her element here as she has it all." Mrs. Gamble, wife of Sir Harcourt Butler's Private Secretary, came to stay to accompany the *prima donna*. Mrs. Gamble had once been accompanist to Tetrazzini and was a pianist of a standard not easy to find in India.

> October 11th. Dame Nellie sang to us on Friday, just a small gathering, and ended up with "Home, Sweet Home". I don't think there was a dry eye in the room and I felt as if another verse would send us all sobbing. On the 10th, H.E.'s birthday, she arranged a programme. All the people who loved music, all those who had helped me in various branches of my work, the Doctors, the Nurses, the Welfare Workers, came and it really was a wonderful evening, such as Simla has never seen before.

Finally, to round off this busy second season, she tells the following anecdote:

On the dining-room walls hang shields with Viceroys' coats-of-arms and mottos. H.E.'s *Aut nunquam tentes aut perfice* ('only be content with the highest') was translated by a young soldier as: "Do not live in tents for privacy".

Whose tongue was in whose cheek?

CHAPTER X

The Mahratta States

"Har! Har! Mahadeo!"

War-cry of the Mahrattas.

THE winter of 1922–3 opened with visits to Indore and Gwalior. In spite of her ignorance of Indian history and customs, Alice Reading conveys in her letters the difference of atmosphere from Rajasth'an. After a country of legend and romance, she found herself in an environment reminiscent of the Border Ballads, or the intrigue and bloodshed of the Wars of the Roses. The family of Shivaji the Great, the founder of Mahratta power, dwindled away in the third generation after his death (1680) and the leadership of the Mahratta Confederacy fell into the hands of the Peshwas, hereditary prime-ministers, who held it till 1818, son succeeding father. Maharajah Scindia of Gwalior, Maharajah Holkar of Indore[1] and the Gaekwar of Baroda, the three principal leaders of Maharashtra, were descended from soldiers of fortune who served the Peshwas in the eighteenth century. As the Peshwas, whose headquarters were at Poona, waned, the individual chieftains waxed in power and for a time they all combined in the dream of a Hindu Raj to replace the crumbling Moghul Empire. Unfortunately, this dream had to be abandoned because the chieftains could not agree among themselves. To the Mahratta of those days the end which he was pursuing was always much more important than the means, the end being usually plunder or the aggrandisement of one particular individual. All over Central India and the Deccan and especially in the Western Ghats between Bombay and Poona, immense crumbling fortresses tell the story of Mahratta skill and courage in battle. The confederacy created few contributions to the arts or architecture such as are found in Rajasth'an but the Mahratta Brahmin, from which caste the family of the Peshwas derived, was and is an individual of peculiar intellectual skill and subtlety and a brilliant organiser and administrator.

The rulers of Gwalior and Indore shared a history of constant conflict against each other and it was due to the defection of Holkar's troops that the Mahrattas lost the third battle of Panipat, outside Delhi (January, 1761), when they fought an Afghan, Ahmed Shah Durrani, who had control at that time of the enfeebled descendant of the great Akbar.

At the time of the Readings' visit, Indore was a flourishing state, the chief mart for Central India and a cotton-producing and milling area.

October 25th and 26th. A very interesting week but not as successful as it ought to have been owing to H.E.'s indisposition. He is better now but has been in bed the whole time since day of arrival with a gastric attack. In his place I have been visiting Colleges, Schools, Hostels, Hospitals, 2 official dinners and a garden party, in between tucked in bed with all the fans on as heat in middle of the day very great.

I started with a visit, with the Maharajah, to the State Hospital. He, the Maharajah, is a peculiar fellow with an enormous sense of his great dignity. He had an exhibition of the manufactures of Indore arranged for me, there are wonderful cotton factories here, they turn out shirtings, muslins and calicoes as good as Manchester.

The gentleman[2] who owns most of them wears a calico garment with a tape round his waist and 8 rows of huge priceless pearls under his muslin shirt. He also wears a watch chain of pearls like filberts. I won his heart by asking to see his factory and we went this morning, the whole place ablaze with bunting and Welcomes. Quite the most interesting of my jobs was the opening of a Training school for teachers to be named after me. The kiddies are taught by Montessori methods and it seemed so strange to me to see the little bits of work and weaving done by my grandchildren repeated here in the wilds of Central India. All the little ones in bright coloured saris like tropical birds, each with a little flag. Next day another Hospital and a visit to a charming little private Nursing Home kept by French Nuns for Europeans and Eurasians. They were such dears and lived such wonderful lives all for the good of others, we came away feeling the better. I tried to get out of the Resident what I would give them and at last they confessed they could not work so much at night as they had no good lamp, so the best lamp Calcutta can produce shall go to lighten their lives.

On this trip the Readings were accompanied by Mr. John Thompson,[3] Political Secretary to the Government of India, the department in charge of the State affairs. As Yvonne FitzRoy says:

... there is nothing in the Indian heaven or on the Indian earth or under it of which Mr. Thompson has not a wealth of stories to tell. He likes history but he also likes the fantastic and he can read Persian. He will tell you the thrilling story of how the Maharajah Scindia of Gwalior found treasure worth two million sterling on his back stairs!

The garden party took place at the Daly College, a school for the sons of Mahratta Princes and noblemen. "There are four 'houses'," says Yvonne, "and at one end of the ground a mosque presented by the Begum of Bhopal, at the other a Hindu temple."

Alice Reading describes going to and fro in crowded streets, the main colours a blaze of orange and scarlet, " . . . if it were not for H.E.'s indisposition it would be wonderful, but as it is I am wearing myself out." However, she is able to write on her arrival at Gwalior:

> The end of our stay at Indore was most successful and quite made up for the beginning as H.E. gave the young Maharajah of Rewa[4] his full powers instead of our going the long journey there as we first intended.
>
> On the Sunday I asked the Resident to take me to the poor quarters in the Bazaar and Market. He said, "no Vicereine has ever been there," so I answered, "let me be the first." I went and had an enormous reception, the people came out like rabbits from every hole and hut clad in the most marvellous oranges and crimsons or nothing at all. Prettiest was a little girl of about five with a nose-ring and necklace of silver—nothing else. When I got half-way I said, "We must bring H.E. here," and back I went to fetch him. We stopped at two Mosques, one belonging to the Jain sect, they are people who never take life of insect, beast or bird. They eat no green vegetables for fear of drowning a slug or caterpillar by washing and when they walk they have a sweeper in front of them for fear of treading on an ant.

She persisted in using the term "Mosque" impartially for Hindu and Muslim places of worship throughout her time in India. It may be that her subconscious stopped short at the word "Temple" as a milieu for graven images.

The Jains were a sect of Hindu affiliations but one feels that with the understanding courtesy of the East they would blandly brush aside the assumption that they worshipped in a Mosque, taking Alice Reading for what she gave out in friendliness and interest rather than blaming her for inaccuracy. Indians had a great deal to put up with from the British, the ladies especially, with regard to mistakes in terminology and unintentional rudeness because of faulty attempts to speak Indian languages. The constant mocking of "Babu English" on our part had no counterpart that we were ever allowed to hear, though no doubt in the privacy of Indian homes some strange stories were told of unfortunate things we said or did.

Alice Reading's reaction to the temples she entered is interesting. What she found was very similar to the enormously rich and decorated statues of the Virgin and Saints to be seen in Spanish and Italian churches where riches laid upon wood and stone contrast oddly with the poor and worn faces turned up to pray. She was received by —

... my friend the cotton spinner. The mosques were full of Bohemian glass. The huge Gods, one of black marble and one of white, very like Buddhas. There was a side shrine with an elephant's head. Before the images were huge tables of solid silver all with silver cups and flagons as votive offerings — all to a block of marble!

From Indore to Gwalior to stay with Maharajah Scindia, a delightful person, gay, bold and inventive with a real, if impish sense of humour. He possessed all the best Mahratta qualities and was also an excellent and enlightened ruler. The journey from Indore took the Viceregal party into a cooler climate as the way wound up hill and Her Ex. reports:

... two blankets and an eiderdown did not suffice. This Palace (Jai Bilas) looks exactly like the Place Vendôme and is almost the same size. The house itself is nearly all marble with an immense Durbar Hall of gold with yellow curtains. Masses of silver standing about all uncleaned (nearly always so in India), miles of glass chandeliers in ruby and white glass. Even the staircases have glass rails and newels.

The Maharajah is a dear, so jolly and friendly. He took us to see a wonderful garden and confided in me the only flower he knew was the eucalyptus plant! He has a craze for mechanical toys. At the Banquet a miniature railway runs round the table with food and drink on it. He is a great potentate and everyone has a good word for him even if it were only for the record of "What Gwalior did in the War".

Writing a week later she gives a further description of the famous toy train on the dinner table:

At a given signal the silver train ran down the rails with a large silver engine, trucks with decanters of port, etc., and trucks filled with sweets. As you took the decanter or sweet out, the train stopped, as you replaced it the train started. It is the only such train in the world.

The next day a splendid review of the Gwalior troops. H.E. rode and took the salute while Mary, aged 8, and George, aged 6, children of the

Maharajah, marched in khaki at head of their regiments. Mary, the
Queen's god-daughter, wears full khaki uniform with a pigtail hanging
down. George is sweet, the image of the dear Maharajah, always a broad
smile not to say grin. I went and paid the two Maharanees a visit. The
eldest is almost 40 and has no children, so she chose No. 2, the mother of
the boy and girl. No. 1 is about 3 feet high, very clever, very charming.
No. 2 dull and not well educated but she had a bilious attack, poor thing!

Mahratta ladies have always been exceptionally emancipated and gay,
and in the history of both Gwalior and Indore, female rulers hold a
proud place. Mahratta women used to ride in battle with their lord,
and go hawking and hunting also. They wear their saris quite differently from anyone else in India, the tail of the sari being brought
up between the legs to make the whole garment into a sort of culottes.
This is not as graceful as the usual fashion but much more practical.
In the early part of the nineteenth century an Englishwoman called
Fanny Parkes wrote an enthralling book about her "wanderings in
search of the picturesque during 24 years in the East". She always
visited Indian ladies of every community and spoke several dialects
fluently. She describes a visit to a Gwalior Maharanee of those days
and an exhibition of European horsemanship which she gave to the
assembled company. The Mahratta ladies were convulsed with merri-
ment and scorn at the fashion of riding side-saddle and they insisted
that Fanny Parkes should jump up astride and gallop around as they
did.

By November 9th, the Viceregal party returned to Delhi and to the
usual round of work and entertainment. Her Ex. lent Maharajah Alwar
Coué's book which so impressed that gentleman that he said he would
visit the Coué establishment at Nancy on his way to England. Her Ex.
opened a hostel at the Lady Hardinge College planned for an Indian
Nurses' Hostel, the first of its kind in India. She talks of fund-raising
for lepers and ends up her letter of November 30th:

> ... A cheque for 17,000 rupees just arrived for my Fund, which now stands
> at a large sum. I need it all, poverty indescribable.

She was thinking much about Calcutta and it is incongruous to read
of the European life there, the hectic pursuit of pleasure when
appalling distress pervaded the poor quarters. But alongside the
racing and dancing and polo, efforts were being made to meet what has
proved to be an insoluble problem even now the British have gone.

Nothing is sadder than Pandit Nehru's[5] assumption in a book written from prison[6] that if only the British could be pushed out there would be no more famine, no more disease, no more poverty, no more over-crowded housing, no *lathi* charges, injustice and so on. A significant alteration in the manner of life of the British could not have raised more than a pin-head of extra money for the immense poverty of India. The sahibs and memsahibs danced and played, most of them at least, to take their minds off problems larger than life which they knew neither they nor anyone else could solve in a day. Meanwhile the Inchcape Committee sat in Delhi trying to retrench and at the end of their day's work they danced and played with the rest.

Just before leaving for Calcutta, Lady Reading records sadly:

> I have had to renounce a very amusing entertainment. Sir Edwin Lutyens had arranged a visit for me to New Delhi. They run a light railway for bricks and stones from the kiln to the new Palace. This was to be "sump-shusly" decorated for me with scarlet bunting and armchairs, 2 similar trucks for Aides and household behind. We were to halt at various points of interest, tea was to be served, his staff presented, all sorts of jokes dear to his heart were to be played, now alas! I have to give it up so as to be ready for my journey. It would have been a wonderful change from all the pomp and ceremony and great fun.

On the way to Calcutta the Viceregal train stopped in Patna, the capital of Bihar and Orissa, then a newly-formed province with a new Government House, one of the most comfortable in India:

> Rice is peculiarly bad in India, on the principal that you can get no good Gruyère cheese in Switzerland. Patna is the only place for good rice and I propose taking a sack back with me.
>
> December 14th. Calcutta again. It seems so incredible a year has gone by since we were here last. H.E. and I gazed rapturously at a tram last night and got quite excited at the outside view of the Army and Navy Stores. I can't help contrasting our visit to Calcutta this year with last. H.E. and I were worried to death over the Prince's visit, Gandhi business, general unrest. Now, thank God, a wonderful peace reigns. The belief in H.E. grows every day. It is a comfort to think this year has not been lived in vain. We have both had a wonderful year. I shall never be thank-ful enough we came to India. It is a marvellous experience. We are going to have our new Air Force where we live now, Simla and Delhi. So do not be surprised if I fly over for a week-end. The Air Marshall tells me in a very short time we shall receive and send letters in under a week!

7

The Viceroy backed two outsiders at the races and won what was said in the bazaars to be an enormous sum of money, a very popular win in a gambling and betting community.

A dream, or rather nightmare, of Hospitals, Homes and Christmas shopping marred by being tucked into bed by Sister at odd moments. A lovely outing to Botanical Gardens with a short trip in the Government launch.

So it went on to the end of the year, with a final State Ball for 800:

It's rather an ordeal as people crowd gallery and all round and make remarks. One gentleman (?) remarked of Lord Lytton [Governor of Bengal], "Why doesn't he unbutton his face?" He always looks, and is, very solemn and is always my partner. Tomorrow 2,000 garden party, am thankful to say everyone going for a river trip on Sunday and I shall be left behind to collect my scattered senses and try and thank for my Christmas presents. The Chinese shoemaker sent me a Christmas card, the Indian silk merchant from Simla one "with love and best wishes".

On January 8th, 1923, Yvonne FitzRoy notes:

We left Calcutta after dinner, an exhausted company. But at least all Her Ex. has been and done has, I think, been appreciated.

DELHI, January 10th. Delhi is heavenly. Sweet-peas, roses, and thunderstorms!

CHAPTER XI

Infinite Variety

"Jaisa des waisa bhes — Every country hath its own fashions."

Indian Proverb

THE year 1923 opened in a calmer political atmosphere. The "Swaraj" party, formed by Pandit Motilal Nehru[1] and Mr. C. R. Das,[2] broke away from Mr. Gandhi's Non-Co-operation movement and decided to contest elections to the Legislative Assembly. This was done with a view to "wrecking from within" but at least the Montagu-Chelmsford Reforms stood some chance of implementation and Indians took part, in however small a way, in the government of their country and gained some parliamentary experience. The economic situation stabilised and above all there had been a good monsoon. On the debit side there was trouble brewing in the Punjaub, due to the rise of the militant Akali movement among the Sikhs and, during the year, the setting-up of a Royal Commission led by Lord Lee of Fareham[3] disturbed and inflamed Indian opinion. The Commission's main purpose was to look into the grievances of the Indian Civil Service and the Police and to revise conditions of pay and service. Indian opinion saw in this benefits for Europeans at the expense of the people of India.

Alice Reading, during this year, shows a marked increase in confidence and authority. Her first interest was the forwarding of her husband's career, her second the work she felt it a duty — and joy — to do for the people of India. She had reason to feel, in 1923, that both interests were advanced.

At the same time her health seems to have been more precarious than ever and she shows signs of physical strain. The hectic Christmas at Calcutta left her very low, with neuritis and rheumatic troubles sufficient to keep her in her room for some time.

January 25th. My hand-writing is more illegible than usual as my hand is still stiff. It is getting better but cold winds still continue and these are

bad for neuritis. H.E. and some men are dining quietly together and playing bridge and I am writing by a nice wood fire in my own pretty room.
Since I have been ill I have shirked dinner and only gone in on guest
nights. I went for my first drive to-day since Calcutta, to a Moghul garden
quite close by here with hundreds of almond trees in bloom. We robbed
the garden in a most un-Viceregal manner, came back laden with great
boughs of blossom in January!

On 30th I open the first Indian Nursing Home (i.e. Home for Nurses)
to be known as the Lady Reading Hostel. The nurses look so nice in blue
and white ginghams. I am quite proud of the first four Indians, they
complete their training in the Wards and are getting better pay and better
quarters and food than Indians have ever had before so we get better-class
women. In the near future we are hoping to get Hindu Widows, poor little
creatures, they marry often at 12 years old and if their husbands die are
not allowed to re-marry, their life is done and they are kept apart with no
work and no future, so these girls we are trying to educate and train.[4]
Already one large Training College is opened and we are following this
on, but work is enormous and I have so many irons in the fire and so short
a time to do it all. A Viceroy ought to stop out 10 years, and go home every
third year for 6 months holiday.

Yvonne FitzRoy describes the opening of the Hostel:

To-day Her Ex., "with her well-known bonhomie and charm" (*vide* a
Calcutta weekly) opened the Lady Reading Hostel at the Lady Hardinge
College. Personally I considered the charm much in evidence, and those
who wish to test the bonhomie have only to produce a lakh or two—the
effect is instantaneous! But it was a great function attended by many of
the country's Legislators (the House was adjourned for the occasion) and
by no less a person than our old friend Sir Hukum Chand, in white muslin,
pearl watch chain and emeralds. The Hostel is a very fine building and
would never have been added but for Her Ex.

In February the Spring tour took the Viceregal party to Ajmere and
Jodhpur in Rajasth'an and then to visit the Nawab of Rampur, a
Muslim state in what is now called Uttar Pradesh. Ajmere was a small
enclave of British India right in the middle of Rajasth'an and perched
on a pinnacle of the jagged Aravalli Range. The Viceroy went to
present prizes at the Mayo College for the sons of princes and noblemen, an extremely efficient school sometimes known as the Eton of
India. However, it differed in some respects, notably in the retinue
which each pupil brought with him suited to his rank and riches.
Yvonne writes:

In the front row (at the Prize-Giving) of the audience sat the eleven
year old Maharajah of Jaipur, fat, sulky and magnificent, while the pupils
of the College were ranged in a circle round the platform. Delicious little
boys in silk and brocade and wonderful jewels. The front row was reserved
for those who had acted as mounted escort to H.E. They clattered in
later looking refreshingly business-like in their khaki uniforms with
puggarees[5] of the five colours of Rajputana wound round their heads. Gay
puggarees too for they are of orange-blue-yellow-white and green. Though
the school, situated where it is, necessarily draws its recruits chiefly from
the great Rajput families, yet others come from all parts of India, and
amongst them there was even a little Arab Shaikh from Muscat.

We got back to the Residency in time to see the sunset turn to flame,
the hills to purple, the city to a blue mist and the whole more fantastically
and mediaevally Italian than ever.

After that, on to Jodhpur on the edge of the Bikaner desert, the
capital of Marwar from whence Beekar set out to carve his kingdom
from the sand. There Lord Reading invested the young Maharajah[6]
with full powers and Her Ex. visited the shy, sixteen-year-old Maharani who had given up her private rooms for her guest. Everything was
European,

> ... pale blue silk hangings with lovely dressing and bathrooms with every
> known bath salt and perfume from the Rue de la Paix. Next day we visited
> the Fort which is perfect: high up, carved out of the rocks. We motored
> part of the way and then were carried in red velvet and gold chairs. Up
> top I was met by the chief European ladies in Jodhpur and conducted to
> four more Maharanis, widow and sisters of the predecessor. I wish you
> could have seen the Purdah Courtyard, all carved in white marble like
> alabaster, a circle of chairs, an arm chair in the middle for me, round me
> the Maharanis and ladies. An outer circle of retainers, some young with
> wonderful nose rings, some old, all wrapt in saris of orange, yellow, gold,
> all alive with curiosity.

Lady Reading worried about the lives of purdah ladies; she felt they
must be miserable, but she did not quite understand their compensations. She did not realise that in her own life she, too, observed a form
of purdah and had the same compensations as her Indian sisters of the
princely order. She was utterly secure and protected, honoured as
mother and wife, without material cares and able to wield power without responsibility.

Yvonne FitzRoy makes the point that Jodhpur Fort was the first one
she felt to be—

... very much alive, but with a life centuries old. Gorgeous, embroidered dhoolies[7] awaited and carried us up the narrow, stone-paved ascent, with a high wall on the one hand and the eight storeys of the Palace rising sheer from the rock on the other. From the tremendous masonry beside us to the lovely, carved balconies and windows hanging far above against the narrow ribbon of blue sky— it was perfect. I am told that no less an authority than Sir Edwin Lutyens described it as the most remarkable structural feat in his experience.

Lady Reading writes one of her best letters from Rampur. The Nawab, Sir Mohammed Ali,[8] an engaging character, a friendly, gregarious man, concluded the pact of *"Pagri Badal"* with Harcourt Butler, an exchange of headgear symbolising a tie of brotherhood. Relationships meant a great deal to him, as Alice Reading was to discover:

> After a night's travelling reached Rampur at 8.30 this morning. No-one knows what it means to arrive at such an hour in your best clothes and best smile not to speak of a white dress and *hat* when you have left the age of 30 behind you!
>
> As I write the guns are booming the salute as H.E. is returning the Nawab's visit. I forgot if I told you he, the Nawab, put in a lift for me. When we arrived, lift did not work and we had to stand around for a quarter of an hour while man was found who had turned off the current. I would not be in that man's shoes but I don't suppose he has shoes now, they belong to his widow!!
>
> Another contretemps, a magnificent tent, over 100 years old with silver poles, lent to the King for his Durbar, burnt down last night. The electrician is "doing time". I take tea with the Begum (as Mahommedan Maharanis are called), we see the wonderful Library, then a State Banquet tonight followed by a cinema performance of *"Kismet"*.

By this time Her Ex. is becoming aware of the variation in Indian titles, and the next day she writes of her visit to the Begum who, if not as blue-blooded and correct as the Rajput ladies, was more colourful in character:

> The visit to the Begum was most amusing. She has been a dancer, is quite fascinating but she chews betel nut all day, or rather *"pan"*. 100 a day and will not go to Europe with him as she cannot get the *pan* fresh. She wore a gorgeous dress, enormous pearl tassels in her hair, diamonds through her nose, she had to lift the nose ring every time she drank. The Nawab translated and his sons handed round cakes and sweetmeats. His

daughter-in-law was present, married to the heir. Next to my room was a high brick wall, the Zenana, and there about 100 wives lived, each one in a little flat of about three rooms, with their own servant to prepare their own food as each is afraid of being poisoned by the other.

In the Library he has a marvellous collection of Persian drawings, illuminated manuscripts and books 600 to 700 years old, some of them. He spent the entire time sitting next me at meals trying to trace a common ancestry as Mahommedans are descended from Ishmael. He cross-questioned me as to the habits, ways and lives of Jews and was very upset that Moses' tomb was not better cared for. I was very apologetic and in the end he said to me, "Excellency, does your family date back 500 or 600 years?" I assured him it was so ancient I had lost count! He said it must be in the archives in Jerusalem and urged me to make a pilgrimage there and look it up. I *did* have a time! But I left the old gentleman firmly convinced we were cousins!

Islam, Israel and the Christians are "people of One Book", the Old Testament. The Festival of Bakr-Id in the Muslim faith is the Feast of the Ram and celebrates the saving of Isaac from the sacrificial knife of Abraham. Moses is especially venerated. This episode in Rampur shines agreeably in a divided world. Alice Reading, cosmopolitan, latitudinarian, humorous and courteous, meets the old Nawab half way on ground common to both. She ends this letter on a note of relief:

... the two men have been pardoned, which is a weight off our minds.

Lady Reading returned to Delhi to continuous entertaining for the Chamber of Princes which was in session. The familiar Maharajahs pass through her letters and the catalogue is varied by a visit from:

... The Maharajah of Sikkim and Maharani.[9] She a wonderful little figure in every colour of the rainbow with an attractive Japanese-like face. She wore an enamelled scarlet *fence* round her head with the hair brushed over, with great things dangling of turquoises and pearls, to her waist and the same behind hanging on to her flowing hair [a very neat sketch is inserted at this point]. They were a fascinating couple.

There were a number of American tourists in Delhi at the time and Lady Reading took a curiously assorted party, including Miss Jane Addams, a social welfare worker, and the Maharajah of Alwar (of all people) —

... to my Reading Hostel and left them to assimilate Welfare from my capable Lady Doctor. I felt so pleased when passing through the great

Wards to think I had made them possible by begging for the £20,000 to complete them. The Maharajah of Alwar then and there presented me with the promise of a great shield cut in Alwar marble to commemorate the opening of the Hostel.

Next night a real treat, for thanks to friends at home a band of 3 musicians dined with us and played wonderful violincello, violin and piano trios till their train left. The strains fell on grateful ears; oh! the comfort of sitting in an armchair and listening, instead of making conversation all the time.

Tomorrow we are supposed to be off to Bhopal, to-day an anxious Nurse and Doctor take turns at putting a little thermometer in my mouth. I am quite all right and no doubt by tomorrow shall start off smiling, with a very red nose!

Influenza nearly wrecked the visit to Bhopal, which was sad as she was particularly fond of the Begum. There is always an especial liveliness in any descriptions of this splendid old lady:

The Begum did it all in great style. She goes about in an immense shawl-like garment with a white strawberry basket inverted on her head. In day time it sports a diamond spray, in evening a tiara on top. When the veil is drawn aside a wonderfully shrewd pair of brown eyes is revealed. She would be so handsome if she had not jagged stumps of teeth black from betel nut.

Pan-chewing must be many thousands of years old in Asia; there are records of it as far back as 5,000 B.C. and it is equivalent to smoking or gum-chewing in the West. *Pan* "quids" contain shredded tobacco and spices and always a touch of lime, and all is wrapped in the betel leaf. The red juice comes from the shredded areca nut which is an essential part of the mixture. The whole has a sharp, pleasing, bitter taste and a slightly anaesthetic effect in the mouth. Women regard it as having contraceptive properties whereas it is said to stimulate virility in men. There is no doubt that it carries the danger of oral cancer and certainly stains and destroys the teeth. But these possibilities are no more deterrent than the fear of lung cancer on smoking.

Her Ex. visited the Girls' School, the Purdah Ladies' Club and the Hospital. The Club ladies were all the Begum's poor relations and their ruler remarked tersely: "What I tell them to do, they do, and they are very happy." The Hospital, according to Yvonne, was "rotten", but the Begum announced the building of a new ward. The training of midwives, later to be Lady Reading's chief contribution to social work in India, was still embryonic and the traditional *Dais* at Bhopal did repel with their crone-like and dirty appearance. So would Mrs. Gamp look to us now, were she to present herself at a prize-giving at some modern hospital. Yvonne gives a picture of the Begum relaxed, taking the ladies of the party out to her farm without Her Ex. who was resting:

> The children ran about doing some execution with water pistols whenso-ever Grandmama was *not* looking. When she was, the devil visibly ran out of their toes and left them little pattern Princesses. We wandered about the farm picking oranges off her orange trees and watching oxen draw water from the great Persian well.

As the Viceregal party left a State Banquet for their train, the Begum presented H.E. with a marvellous bag, thick gold embroidery on crim-son velvet. This, she said, was to be his "hunting bag" to take on all his *shikar* trips in the jungle.

A visit to the state of Kapurthala in the Punjaub near the Himalayan foothills, proved to be a considerable contrast. The Maharajah, an unorthodox Sikh who spent most of his time in Europe, did not observe the five "K's" of the Khalsa. He cut his hair and shaved and, as Her Ex. puts it, was "the most European of the Indian Princes". She adds that he was "married to a Spanish dancer but divorced her some years back". King Edward VII is said to have been much annoyed because Kapurthala moved into the same hotel as His Majesty in Biarritz accompanied by the said Spanish dancer, as mistress rather than wife.

Be that as it may, Kapurthala was a most charming man, with a beautiful and charming family. The elder branch became Christian and therefore stood aside from the rulership of the state. Rajkumari Amrit Kaur, Health Minister in the first Indian Government after Independence, was a daughter of the senior branch.

> We had a very pleasant stay at Kapurthala. He is the most charming host, the blend of Parisian and Oriental rather attractive. It is most noticeable in the house. One mass of gold with Nymphs disporting them-selves on vaulted ceilings and innumerable Sèvres ornaments and vases and "objets d'art" about. The first day we had a garden party with splen-did tennis. Sleem, the champion Indian player, beating a Kapurthala man almost equally good. At the back of the garden a Fair with elephants, conjurors, jugglers, fire-eaters and trapeze walkers. The gardens are

beautifully laid out with a background of snow mountains which made the
air delightfully refreshing.

The ladies consisted of a fascinating little daughter-in-law and a newly-
married daughter. One, be-rouged, carmine lips and exquisite sari, looked
like a lovely doll. She fascinated all the men and most of the women. The
daughter a beautiful Indian woman, splendid features, dark skin, with
colour in her cheeks. Both educated in Paris and England. They were very
easy to get on with and looked wonderful at the State Banquet. His
Highness had his Indian cooks taught in Paris, a welcome change. The
Banquet was a very cheery affair.

Next day I visited the school, such a pretty sight, hundreds of kiddies
in coloured saris, they pelted me with flowers all the way from car to
school. Later we went up and down the river in a beautiful Thorneycroft
motor-launch.

Back again in Delhi she writes of a change of plans before the spring
move to Simla. The Maharajah of Gwalior suggested that they should
spend ten days in April in his hunting lodge at Sipri. It happened that
a particularly sudden onset to the hot weather made Delhi seem
dry and scorched. The thought of a jungle hunting lodge beside a lake
greatly appealed to Her Ex. and Lord Reading looked forward to
shooting a tiger. Things did not turn out quite as they had expected
and Alice Reading was the principal sufferer:

10 o'clock at night. I am trying to write as Mail goes tomorrow, but heat
is so terrific we are lying about like flies. In the next room H.E. and 3 moist
and languid people are playing bridge. Every door and window open and
all the electric fans on. The men are carrying tubs of ice to various bedrooms to try and bring the temperature down, and a dozen water carriers
with their skins full of water are trying to cool the marble of the verandah
outside our rooms. We leave tomorrow night for Sipri travelling through
the night and reaching Gwalior at 6 in the morning, then have $2\frac{1}{2}$ hours
motor journey to our destination. The garden here is unrecognizable
since three days, it is just as if a hot blast had struck down each flower
leaving a burnt track behind.

Plague has been pretty bad in Delhi and I could not pay my usual
visits to Health Centres or Infant Welfare for that reason. We are opening
a new Crêche, the first attempted, at New Delhi during these terribly
hot summer months as hundreds of women are engaged in breaking
stones, carrying mortar, etc. for the new Viceregal Lodge, and we want a
place they can leave their babes during the day instead of carrying them
on their backs covered with their loads, in this heat. It is quite an experiment but I am lucky enough to have the funds, and a few splendid Euro-

pean women whose husbands have to remain on here are helping, so I live in hope!

The women with the baskets on their heads helped to build all the Delhis, and they have done the same for Corbusier's Chandigarh even now in this age of mechanisation.

Sipri turned out to be hotter than Delhi. Although slightly higher in altitude it is a good deal further south:

We arrived in Gwalior to find the Light Railway waiting for us with the Maharajah acting as driver. The real driver was sitting on the step and distinguished himself by falling off half-way, Colonel Carey-Evans [Surgeon] having to give First Aid to a cut head. This house is an enormous building with a big balcony with tesselated pavement stretching outside our windows. The heat is indescribable. Impossible to go out in the day time and at night we disport ourselves in various cots on the balcony with the heavens as canopy.

The first night I took my sun umbrella to bed to keep the moon off, but found it came in handy next morning as a signalling party was on the neighbouring parapet. We have to go in when the sun rises as it would be too hot and H.E. had to hold the sun umbrella over most of my anatomy before I could leave my couch. I wish you could have seen us at 5 a.m. clad in the lightest garb, armed with pillows, and flourishing the sun umbrella!

On one of my nocturnal expeditions I went into my room and, instead of grasping the door handle, grasped the electric fan, with the result that my right hand is bound up, although much better.

After this Her Ex. went down with sand-fly fever, a very nasty affliction which induces a high temperature and a feeling of complete collapse. She tells of lying in bed in a dark room while Colonel Carey-Evans thinks up devices for cooling down the hot air. She still contrives to write amusingly of what she hears from the others, and there is no word of complaint or self-pity in this letter from Sipri. It is characteristic of the understanding between her and her husband that he made no change in his plans or expeditions. In various ways, this illness must have had its counterpart in times past and it became an accepted fact between them that if he gave up anything in which he was engaged to be by her bedside, that would only make her feel worse.

On April 1st, the Maharajah left us for the day to attend his sister's memorial service. He fasted all day, according to his religion, but enlivened proceedings by a series of April Fool jokes which gave him immense pleasure. He started off by having salt put in everyone's morning tea, with the exception of H.E.'s and mine, served poached eggs made of china for breakfast and sent me a telegram telling me the Maharani was ill and would be grateful for my enquiries. Sister had a pillow in her bed that squeaked like a baby, the wafers for the ice were lined with blotting paper, all the lights were turned out and various other pranks which one can only connect with a schoolboy. His enjoyment of all these jokes makes him most loveable. He has a wonderful flair for machinery, drives a train and his cars and steers his own ship.

Yvonne FitzRoy gives a very interesting description of the mausoleum the Maharajah made for his mother, whom he had greatly loved. In it he placed a marble statue of her which was attended by female servants who dressed and undressed the image and waved fans to keep her cool. A band played from time to time, and the Maharajah built a pavilion nearby in which he entertained guests who were *her* guests, and where he would go to rest and relax in her company. Yvonne records that she and others were not at all disturbed by the atmosphere of the place, but convinced of a certain cheerfulness and healthiness of approach to death which carried a lesson in it. She uses the expression, "the high sanity of his faith. He has visualised the lasting things of memory, and this with no sacrifice of either dignity or regret."

The Viceroy saw five tigers and shot two, one of which was swimming in the river. It was a rash and difficult shot to take and the animal had to be followed up. But it proved to be a record. Lord Reading greatly enjoyed his jungle visits. He mentioned them especially in his farewell speech to the princes before he left India. They were a new experience in his strenuous life; he had little time to spare in the past for the relaxations of the chase and he appreciated them all the more for coming to them late in life. They also gave him a chance to establish camaraderie and confidence with his hosts.

CHAPTER XII

The Third Round

"Let us go over to the Simla Club. Lights are gleaming from the long row of windows in the bungalow. Syces holding horses and jampanis sitting in groups are clustering round the Verandah. Servants are hurrying to wait on the Sahibs who have come to dinner from distant bungalows."

W. H. Russell, Correspondent of *The Times*, on a visit to Simla, 1859.

A POLITICAL crisis came to a head just before the Viceroy's holiday at Sipri.

The first session of the Legislative Assembly for 1923 showed little sign of Parliamentary responsibility. Each item that came up for discussion received rough treatment from the Swarajists as a matter of principle, oblivious of its intrinsic merit. The budget met with especial obstruction. Sir Basil Blackett,[1] the Finance Member, contrived a brilliant reconstruction of India's tottering finances. He anticipated a surplus of $2\frac{1}{2}$ crores (over 2 million sterling) for 1924–25. With this surplus he proposed to reduce the Salt Tax, a measure of the utmost benefit to the poorest classes. The disposal of the surplus, left to the vote of the Assembly, was systematically rejected by the Nationalist bloc. Finally, in spite of being twice presented to the Lower House, the Finance Bill was refused introduction in any form. Lord Reading then used his special powers and sent the Bill to the Council of State where it became law.

At this point in India's constitutional development the Viceroy alone held responsibility for certifying legislation. Lord Reading was the first holder of the office to have to take this responsibility. Under the Montagu-Chelmsford Reforms there was no real party system, and the government was always opposed by a majority opposition. Previously, with only a limited number of elected seats, government could always be sure of a majority. It was Lord Reading's task, and he accomplished it triumphantly, to govern constructively and peacefully throughout an unprecedented period of political transition.

Lady Reading understood her husband's problems though she was never a woman who "played politics". From this time onwards her letters tend to lose their note of naïvety and diffidence. She became more entrenched in her position and less accessible to ordinary people.

> May 2nd, 1923. We are up at Mashobra. I vegetate! The weather is gorgeous, as I write on the verandah hundreds of different coloured butterflies come and stare at me, the Iris are all in bloom and the woods look lovely from my balcony. Every now and again the tinkle-tinkle of bells breaks the silence and a procession of mules laden with our food for to-day and to-morrow wends its way up the path. Every few hours a vision of scarlet and gold appears, a tall Bodyguard on a coal black horse carries despatches, telegrams, letters. What I like least, every now and again a Coolie appears with an enormous load on his head. I have tried in vain to stop it, have inaugurated luggage waggonettes, mule transport, etc. but so they will live and die in India. We had a very sad farewell just before leaving Simla for the biggest Bank there closed its doors the day we came away, there was terrible consternation amongst the entire public, military and civilian. Fortunately creditors will be paid half at once but all sorts of exaggerated stories of ruin were carried from mouth to mouth. It will cast a gloom over Simla, already none too well off. It is difficult in many cases to make both ends meet with a family of children at home to educate and support.

The Alliance Bank of Simla closed its doors early in the month very soon after the pay of government officials and army officers had been paid into their accounts, so real hardship ensued. It is too often assumed that, because the British in India had many servants and enjoyed good sport, shaking of the Pagoda Tree continued after the eighteenth century. But Alice Reading is right when she says that the British in Simla were none too well off. Living was cheap, so was labour, but pay was small, especially in the army and in the lower grades of the civil service. Until the Lee Commission decreed some help for sea passages home the cost of these had to be met from private means, and the expense of two households in the hot weather also made a big hole in the pay packet. Alice Reading, none too well off in her early married life, could understand this but she was critical of English women in Simla because they did little social work. The difficulty was that such work, like everything else, had to be based on precedence. If the Colonel's wife and the Commissioner's wife did not take the lead, lesser women got no opportunity.

The shadow of the bank failure lay over the hills and Alice Reading decided to cheer everyone by a special party. This is her account of it:

> The Moonlight Revel was the creation of a fevered brain. I had thought of
> it when I had sand-fly fever. It was a success, I must say. 800 people
> revelled and danced. Many threw off the cares of state who had been old
> men for years and became young again at the Old English Fair. I wore a
> gold Callot dress, pannier fashion, we were the only people not in fancy
> dress. The entire lawn had white canvas stretched which was waxed and
> powdered, and surrounded by tubs of hydrangeas, at the back festoon
> after festoon of red, white and blue electric lights. A full moon, the entire
> garden surrounded by walls of Dorothy Perkins in full bloom, all this
> made a fairyland of the scene. The Old English Fair had booths, merry-
> go-rounds, baked potato stall, freaks, Aunt Sally, fortune tellers and sur-
> prises and prizes galore. If you had seen grave Indians, Council of State
> members, up and down on the see-saw and merry-go-round, you would
> not have believed your eyes. But the "clou" of the entertainment was the
> sight of the Viceroy, Governor of the Punjaub and the Commander-in-
> Chief going down the shute together. Then the three of them repaired
> to the hot potato stall and ate chips and baked potatoes as if they were
> school boys. The surprise of the evening was an elephant with mahout,
> which proceeded to "salaam" in front of our tent and trumpet the most
> terrible noises, then made a charge at the Military Secretary.[2] This all a
> skit on an adventure we had at Sipri when a real elephant went for him
> and he had to run for his life. It ended by the "elephant" going down the
> shute, and then we left the young people (and old) who kept it up till 3
> in the morning!

Lady Reading's letter from the Frontier in April, 1922, mentions
Mrs. Starr, Matron of a Mission Hospital at Peshawar, who now
became the heroine of a grim adventure. On April 13th, 1923, an
Afridi tribesman murdered Mrs. Ellis, wife of a British staff officer and
abducted her daughter as a hostage for his own safety. Mrs. Starr
volunteered to go across the Frontier and parley with the murderer
for the return of the girl. She was an accomplished Pushtu speaker,
known and beloved all over the area for her work in the hospital at
Peshawar. It will be remembered that her own husband had also been
murdered by an Afridi. She achieved the release of Miss Ellis without
any concessions given in return.

On July 5th, Lady Reading writes with real emotion:

> Such a wonderful evening last night when H.E. decorated Mrs. Starr and
> the 2 Indian officers who helped to rescue Miss Ellis. It was proposed to
> have an informal Investiture just after lunch as Mrs. Starr is staying here,

but I objected and was allowed my own way, so I just got up a little dinner of 40 people for her. Sir John Maffey[3] is staying here and several of the Border officials and I invited several prominent Indians because their fellow Indians were to be honoured. Then after dinner we had about another 40 for the Investiture, a lot of Indians, all the Nurses and Sisters and several people doing big work in Simla. Mrs. Starr is the first person to have the Gold Kaisar-i-Hind[4] Medal *with* Bar at the same time. After dinner we all went to the Council Chamber and H.E. pinned it on. She has a sweet little serene face and a lovely expression. In her little black dress she looked about 20. She curtsied with the tears rolling down her cheeks and I knew she was thinking of her murdered husband. I admire her so enormously for she takes her religion into her daily life and is a real little Saint. The Indian soldiers loved it, they took it in turns to sit next to me and converse. They had never been to Viceregal Lodge before. It was a wonderful evening and will live long in our memories and I am glad I had a lot of *young* Indians there to see.

I am promising myself to take Mrs. Starr to my hospital this afternoon, but everything is covered in mist.

It was stimulating for Her Ex. to take someone like Mrs. Starr to the beloved hospital. They could have a really meaningful discussion of things that mattered; nurses' quarters, surgical instruments, how to make the doctor's house comfortable, how to manage the families of Indian patients who came into the wards to sit round the beds day and night. On such an occasion and with such a companion, one can imagine Alice Reading lighting up and certainly not using her elegant tortoise-shell ear-trumpet as frequently as she did when listening to the nervous comments of guests who were led up to her at dinner parties and who found the said ear-trumpet a great discouragement. It was a beautiful work of art in jewelled tortoiseshell and enhanced her style and presence, as well as her aloofness. She writes sadly on July 11th:

Mrs. Starr left us with great regrets on both sides. She is a singularly charming and unspoiled person with a wonderful faith that is enviable. These Mission Hospitals do untold good in India and you find them everywhere in the most benighted regions with just a few, perhaps 2 or 3 wonderful men and women who spend their lives ministering to the sick; their hospitals are staffed by Indian youths who have been converted to Christianity, no nurses, just Doctors and a Matron (as Mrs. Starr is) and their money to run the hospital comes nearly all from England. Mrs. Starr and I got on splendidly and had some most useful conversations on running hospitals.

The Maharajah of Patiala on horseback

The Mall and the Town Hall, Simla

The road to "The Retreat", Mashobra

Lukka Bazaar, Simla

Lady Reading records various illnesses during the rest of the month
—she arose from a diet of "slops only" to come to a big dinner party.
There was her birthday party, with charades put on by the staff, a
big reception for the Legislative Assembly, the official opening ceremony of the Maharajah of Bharatpur's[5] Simla house, a very rewarding
visit from the Thakur of Morvi[6] (45,000 rupees for the hospital), a
Purdah Party at Lady Shafi's (Indian music) and a Purdah Party of her
own at which a "mother of 20" recited an Ode in Urdu in Her Ex.'s
praise. In between she managed some games of pingpong at which she
usually won and also dancing lessons since she felt that the style of her
youth was not equal to the new Viceregal Jazz Band. On August 7th, a
tea to all the teachers in Simla schools, followed by the film of *Little
Lord Fauntleroy*:

> ... I persuaded H.E. to see one or two reels and at the end the Head
> teacher said to him pityingly: "I am afraid, Your Excellency, you felt the
> film was very personal." At first I could not think what she meant, then
> realised it was the "wicked Earl" she alluded to. You can imagine H.E.'s
> face!!
>
> We have again been plunged into mourning by President Harding's
> death. My old black satins are getting very worn. I knew the Vice-Presi-
> dent when I was in America, it is a great burden for any man to take on his
> shoulders, but—how about India? H.E.'s work is never-ending but
> (D.G.) he keeps well on it and is able to throw off his burden at night and
> enjoy his bridge, film, etc. To let you into a secret, he and I are starting
> dancing lessons. There is a *young* class at the Commander-in-Chief's,
> everyone between *40 and 60*, so we are not going to be outdone.
>
> Owing to illness, I missed the "Black Hearts" Ball which was tragic as
> it is one of the few evenings when H.E. and I can do as we like. He selects
> his own partners among the prettiest girls and I have a "Black Heart" for
> every dance and need not *make* conversation. All the eligible bachelors
> belong, and grass widowers who are the gayest of the gay.

"The Most Hospitable Order of Knights of the Black Heart" was
founded in Simla in 1891. In abeyance during World War I, it revived
in 1920. There was always much speculation, especially among women,
about the missing word in the motto of the Order: "He is not so ... as
he is Black." This mystery word was supposed to be set in the heart-
shaped locket that each Knight carried round his neck when in the
picturesque uniform they wore at their Revels—evening dress with
knee-breeches and black silk stockings, a knee-length scarlet cloak

8

with a Black Heart over the left breast and a red band round the left knee. There were never more than 24 Knights and they were appointed by their fellows, the qualification for membership being that no Knight "should be living in open matrimony". If a grass widower's wife returned to him he was allowed to attend functions in the uniform, his red knee-band replaced by white and no collar badge, for he had "lost his Heart". When any matter had to be decided, "the will of the minority prevailed in the interests of harmony". Thus any one Knight could veto any item on the agenda or guest on the list. This did seem to promote harmony for, as Lady Reading says, they were the gayest of the gay and their parties the best in the world. These gatherings took place three times in the season in the covered tennis court at the U.S. Club, disguised by "trappings" and decorations. One revel was always Fancy Dress and they also gave a splendid Children's Party. The girls of Simla enjoyed dancing with the Viceroy because he was the Viceroy and also a most attractive man who did not need dancing lessons at all. When the Prince of Wales visited Delhi, the Black Hearts brought their trappings down from Simla and gave him a party, making him an Honorary Knight, for which permission had to be solemnly asked of King George V.

> August 29th. Only a Ball to chronicle this week, I am afraid I did not see much of it as I only went down for a quarter of an hour. It was remarkable for the fact that I wore a new dress, gold tissue shot with mauve and all embroidered in bullion, the gift of the Nawab of Rampur who had it embroidered for me. On Monday morning I had "avalanched" on me we were going to hold a "Baby Week"[7] in January for the whole of India, and begging me to set the ball rolling, which meant many interviews and more letters. It is rather a big proposition for the whole of this vast country but our organisation is good. By now I have many letters from Governor's wives saying they are ready and willing to help. We live in an atmosphere of flap which reminds me of war days. As one of the Commissioners said to me the other day: "It's a mercy so many of the poor little beggars die, there is no welcome for them especially if female, and there is not enough food to go round as it is." Sad, but true, but we have got to make an effort especially in Bengal where the death rate is incredibly high.

The Commissioner's remark was often repeated to those who worked for India's mothers and babies and it has an especial poignancy to-day, when the problem is still unsolved, for all the hopes expressed by Indians that once the British left, starvation and over-population would vanish too. Without the pioneer work done by Lady Reading and others in Child Welfare, the next step — population control — would have been more difficult to introduce to illiterate parents.

In early September Harcourt Butler and his lively staff arrived from Burma — six day's journey. His naturally high spirits were dimmed by gout but by the end of his visit he was well able to join in an unusual party. What were known as "Harcourt's Hymn Books" had somehow got lost on the journey but arrived just in time for a copy to be available for each of the Viceregal house-party and a selection of Maharajahs. The "Hymns" were mostly hits from the *Co-optimists* and other current London successes.

> "I'm tickled to death I'm single,
> "I'm tickled to death I'm free . . ."

warbled the much-married Maharajahs. Her Ex. went to bed early and seems rather glad she did so:

> They all congregated in the Ball-room when we thought all but the house-party had gone. H.E. went down again while they sang Choruses with Mrs. Gamble at the piano.
>
> There were three highly orthodox Hindu Princes celebrating in song the supremacy of "The Roast Beef of Old England." I cannot say much for the choice of songs and cannot help feeling glad I was not there.

The party succeeded because of absence of self-consciousness on everyone's part. Many British people, with the very best intentions, were over-courteous to Indians. They had one law for the East and one for the West in social relations and soothed their uneasiness with extra tact. A uniform standard of behaviour, of courtesy and discourtesy, has grown slowly with Independence. Harcourt Butler had no doubts about strong government but he was completely natural as between man and man. He once advised a young civilian: "The most important thing is to be accessible, to be not an official only but a friend." Harcourt Butler "was not particularly concerned about democracy or freedom but he was concerned that people should be cheerful and enjoy themselves."[8]

Alice Reading was also concerned that people should be cheerful and enjoy themselves, so she set out to convert a Girl Guide Rally into a real party for a large contingent of British children who came to Viceregal Lodge from the Sanawar Military Orphanage:

We are in the throes of preparation for feeding and housing for 2 days a large contingent of Girl Guides with strict injunctions from their officers they are to have the plainest of fare. Surreptitious efforts on my part to give them meringues and ices for some of the poor little kiddies have not been indulged in that way.

A week later. They came prepared to rough it and sleep on the floor of the Council Chamber but I had a surprise for them, had arranged large Dormitories and they had their meals in state in the Council Chamber, terribly impressed by the scarlet and gold servants who waited on them. The day of the Rally dawned the hottest and most cloudless of days, a royal blue sky and everyone in jubilant spirits. The "Gemma Hailey" [Gemma Hailey, daughter of Sir Malcolm Hailey, Governor of the Punjaub, had recently died and this shield commemorated her] shield was beautifully made by the Arts School at Lahore. I was nervous at speaking before so large an audience, Lady Maclagan, Lady Rawlinson, 2 Bishops and lots of clergy, but it went alright. We finished up with an enormous tea (at least they did) and they departed happily at 8 o'clock by train plus sandwiches and the recollection of two days' unique experiences including the meringues and ices which they had never met before.

The Metropolitan (Archbishop) of Calcutta[9] (vulgarly known as "Bakerloo") is staying here. When I asked H.E. why the Metropolitan was coming, he said: "Oh, about a *Bill*" [For the Disestablishment of the Church in India]. Whereupon I answered, "Why don't you pay the poor man?" We told the Metropolitan and His Grace was highly delighted and assured me when he left he hoped he would not be paid, and then he could come again.

This story about the Metropolitan's Bill went the rounds of Simla at the time. It is amusing to find that she told it against herself.

She describes a private view of the Simla Art Show where she was much intrigued by a—

. . . terrible drawing of a widow and weeping child in a church-yard surveying the dear departed's tomb, with this flowery verse on the Stone:

In Memoriam

Bright be the Peace of thy *Sole*
No lovelier spirit than thine
Ever burst from its mortal control
In the orbs of the Blessed to shine.

Nice and fishy, wasn't it? The joke of it was that the Education Secretary (Mr. Montagu Butler[10]) bought it and sent it to me as a present! To which I answered:

Mr. Butler, no praise could be subtler
In fact I am quite overcome
By this gift of In Memorium.

That year they all stayed in Simla till the third week of October
and Alice Reading regretted having to leave as she longed to sit and
watch girders and bricks and tiles piling on to her hospital. H.E. and
some of the staff went out into the hills for a shoot, and though they
were far away by road, those left behind could see the fires of their
camp across the immense valley, and the white tents by day. The
Viceroy returned "copper coloured, a shine on him that you can see
half a mile off", in time for the usual merry party and charades for
his birthday. Her Ex. visited the Simla Baby Welfare Centre and persuaded the Municipality to go half-shares in rebuilding and improving
it. She had tea with the wife of the retiring Quarter-Master-General, a
lady who weighed 20 stone and who "makes cottage loaves with her own
fair hands". They both went to dinner with Sir Narasimha Sarma,[11]
Member of Council for Law and were fascinated by the decoration
of the table done in coloured rice, "very Bakst". There was a last
Garden Party, a visit to a home for aged European ladies, and a school
prize-giving—all in three weeks. This immensely busy season may
well close with Her Ex.'s reflections:

Two and a half years ago we anchored in Bombay harbour, the first step
in India on our road to our great adventure! I expect in another two and
a half years a very old lady and gentleman will totter off the quay with
some wonderful years of work and play behind them. I hope something
has been attempted, something done, but the task is colossal and needs
50 years, not 5!

CHAPTER XIII

North to South

"*Kalandar hai-chi goyad didah goyad* — Whatever the wandering traveller says, he does so from having seen that of which he speaks."

Indian Proverb

ON October 22nd the winter tour started in Lahore, then the capital of the Punjaub. Lady Reading writes:

We started early this morning for the opening of the addition to the Law Courts. We were met by the Chief Justice (Sir Shadi Lal[1]) and all the Judges; all the barristers and some from various provinces sat in a huge tent. It did seem strange to see the Chief Justice in the familiar robes, he had two small Indian boys to carry his train. The whole performance brought back such memories of the Law Courts and my own "Chief"! In the afternoon the Bench and Bar gave a garden party in a heavenly garden with fountains all around. We had tea on an Island in the middle under a tent reached by little old brick paths with pools each side.

These were the Shalimar Gardens built by Shah Jehan, afterwards sadly mutilated by Ranjit Singh,[2] the Sikh ruler of the Punjaub in the nineteenth century, who carried off much of the inlay and marble from the pavilion on the island and used it to decorate the Golden Temple at Amritsar.

Next day Her Ex. received "5 charming Nuns, 2 French, 1 German, 2 English", in charge of the Women's Lunatic Asylum. "Her Ex. talked all three languages at once," says Yvonne, "and left us and the Sisters gasping. I doubt Paris has ever equalled the sartorial achievement of these gallant ladies in their snow-white habits and black veils."

A Purdah Party followed, a drive through the city, visits to a girls' school and to a health centre run by two energetic English ladies, and also the School of Art. Alice Reading wrote from Patiala a few days later:

The last two days at Lahore were killing work as H.E. had gone into the country (to the Canal Colony of Lyallpur) so all the functions fell on my shoulders. We had a wonderful party the night we left in the grounds of Government House, all illuminated. In one part wrestlers and acrobats, stark naked except for loin cloths, their bodies all greased till they shone in the moonlight. They did such trifles as carrying a full grown horse, and five men, etc. On the top of a mound they had a wonderful native dance by the light of a huge bonfire fed with kerosine. We parted at 10.15 and went off by train. I felt I had lost an opportunity. I departed in my best gold brocade dress and high tiara and I might just as well have gone to bed in them as we were met at Patiala at 8.30 next morning by the Maharajah who wore a coat very much like my dress, and his second best Tiara!

The Patiala programme repeated much of what happened at every State visit but in a particularly gorgeous and virile manner, since Sikhs have a way of doing everything on a larger scale than anyone else. At the State Banquet the Maharajah sneezed —

... an immense pearl fell off his collar. I felt inclined to "pepper" him the next night. He read a very good speech, and the Banquet broke up early as they were shooting at 7 next morning. I had a quiet day, just a drive in the jungle ten minutes from the house, and I only saw blackbuck, partridges, jackals and monkeys. The house has taken fifteen years to build. H.E. and I each had marble bathrooms as big as my morning room at Curzon Street. It was a constitutional to walk from your bath to your shower, back to wash your hands or clean your teeth. We left at 6 o'clock amidst hearty cheers from Indian lungs.

The next stop — Lucknow — has been described by a traveller writing in 1965 as a seedy, run-down city. But the Readings went there very soon after Harcourt Butler left; he loved Lucknow and restored to her some of her glory as the capital of the Kings of Oudh. Alice Reading was, in common with many Europeans, chiefly struck by the ruins of the Residency, left as they were after the Mutiny, with the Union Jack still flying. Nobody realised then that the wounds of the Mutiny could not be healed until the Union Jack did come down. Henry Lawrence's[3] epitaph remains:

"Here lies Henry Lawrence who tried to do his duty"

The interpretation may have changed with the years, the principle endures.

At Allahabad, the next stopping place, they were met by an old friend, Sir Grimwood Mears, Chief Judge of the High Court:

Allahabad was en fête: the streets lined with people; arches and banners, bands and cheers. I hear that no Viceroy ever had such a reception. It was all very gay and a great surprise as everyone thought our visit might be a failure. Later in the morning we went to the Law Courts where the Chief Justice spoke and H.E. replied and the Bench and Bar shouted themselves hoarse. The crowds pressed up against the cars just to see H.E., as one said, he had seen plenty of Viceroys but never one who had been Lord Chief Justice as well.

India is a country of lawyers and, in legal centres like Lahore and Allahabad, the community appreciated a famous member of the legal profession, nearer to themselves than the aristocratic Pro-Consuls usually despatched to govern India, who were more at home with Maharajahs than with the intellectuals of the middle-class.

Back in Delhi, Her Ex. had to lie low with a terrible cold:

I am furious, but I suppose I should have had a swollen head anyhow! H.E. says I take up the entire programme these days, so I am giving him a turn now!

Unluckily the cold got worse and developed into influenza, thus very nearly wrecking Alice Reading's time in Udaipur, capital of Mewar, fountain-head of the royal tribes of Rajasth'an, home of the Sooryavansi, Children of the Sun. Udaipur itself is comparatively modern, having been founded by Udai Singh, unworthy son of an ancient line who abandoned the historic fort of Chitor to the armies of the Emperor Akbar in 1567-68. The story of Mewar is born in legend for the royal house claims descent from the god, Rama. At the time of the Readings' visit the especial position of this "Sun" of the Hindus was still unchallenged, though in riches and power many other Princes excelled him. The Maharana's[4] line was fading away even then and under present circumstances may be returning to legend, but it will surely for ever be a legend which Rajputs will cherish in thought even if unable to do so in fact. There are records of immense antiquity and value in the archives of Mewar and no doubt the songs of the ancient bards of Rajasth'an are still sung in the villages of this remote and beautiful territory. Many of these songs tell of Bappa Rawul, the first of the line to hold Chitor, who ascended the *gadi* roughly about A.D. 728. He is said to have died in Persia at one hundred years old, leaving progeny like the sands of the sea. And from that time onwards his people were constantly at war as wave after wave of Islamic invaders poured into India—waves that receded as the centuries passed but always returned until the Moghul dynasty established itself as the Ruler of Hind. The Ranas of Mewar never admitted defeat until the reign of Jehangir, 1606–27, and alone of all the royal houses of Rajasth'an gave no woman of their blood to be married to a Muslim.

Udai Singh founded the city of Udaipur in a small way but it was developed and exquisitely beautified by Rana Juggut Singh (1734–52). He also rebuilt the shattered walls of Chitor. This fortress suffered conquest three times in its history and Rajputs used to swear by "the sin of the sack of Chitor". On each occasion the men put on saffron robes, symbolising death or victory and, closing the gates behind them, went forward to meet the enemy, never to return. Meanwhile, all the women left behind performed the terrible rite of "*Johur*", immolation by fire in the cavern beneath the citadel. In this way they fulfilled a religious obligation, joining their husbands in death, and they also escaped rape and conquest. Outside the main gateways of forts and palaces in Rajasth'an can be seen the imprints of small hands dyed red on the stone. These were left by Rajputnis going forth to commit *suttee* on the funeral pyres of their lords. The British (strongly supported by advanced Indian opinion) put an end to this custom. But in the ancient days of Rajasth'an no woman would have welcomed such interference. They sometimes fought beside their men and had no desire to survive as captives of enemies of an alien faith.

In the Readings' time the last traces of mediaeval custom still prevailed and nowhere more strongly than at Udaipur. Alice Reading writes on November 11th, 1923:

> I spent the time in the train from mid-day Friday till Saturday morning at 10 o'clock when we arrived at Udaipur, in bed trying to Coué myself into the belief, "Yes! We have no influenza!" But the Yeas carried the day and it really has spoilt my stay here. I feel so seedy and am spending to-day in bed again and thus missing many of the beauties of Udaipur. It is a most heavenly spot, the most beautiful, after Agra, I have seen in India. We had a State arrival, the old Maharana on the platform, surrounded by his nobles. His only son and heir is a cripple, and besides he and "Pa" do not agree very well. The old man is splendid and looks like a Persian drawing, and does not talk a word of English. Everything has to be translated. He is too orthodox to eat with us and only comes to "make believe" to drink the King's health and hear his speech read and H.E.'s in return.

Alice Reading accepted orthodoxy of any kind without comment but she was worried by the wiping of the Maharana's eyes with a cheap towel taken out of a gold-embroidered velvet bag, also by a retainer flicking at the Ruler with a check duster as he sat on a gold and velvet chair. She did not, practical and down-to-earth as she was, quite realise that these details were wholly unimportant and that the Maharana had no need to pander to European custom. Colonel Tod, writing in 1823, remarks that the State of Mewar "settled to an isolated existence and preferred political inferiority to sacrifice of principle".[5]

> The lake looked like every tale of fairy-land rolled into one, thousands of lamps, hundreds of temples, cupolas, and marble palaces, with a dark blue velvet sky overhead, bestrewn with stars. We went in a motor launch to the Palace, I in my best tiara and a red nose, and an aching body sustained by aspirin and Malvern water at the Banquet. Then I took to my bed. A marvellous cinnamon and gold quilt has just been plumped onto my bed. As the temp. is about 120 in the shade, quilt is not well thought of but there may be days when I have reached home when I shall be glad to wrap it round me and remember the beauties and sunshine of Udaipur.
>
> November 12th. Am better to-day, up to see a wonderful "Slaves' Garden" with such fountains! Four black minarets each side and on each silver birds spitting forth the fountain water. The Maharana met us, such a picturesque figure. Every male in Udaipur over 11 wears a sword manufactured here.

Her Ex. could not manage a day at Chitor but went out to meet the rest of the party by train and had tea with them.

> As we left the Residency the Bhil[6] soldiers who formed the Guard of Honour gave their famous war cry all down the avenue. It was weird! They blow on their fingers, one by one, and it is taken up all down the line.

Yvonne FitzRoy felt deeply the romance and tragedy of a dying tradition:

> No Rajput State fails to stir the imagination, but Mewar is the stronghold of a tradition so remote and undisturbed as to startle indeed our mushroom vanities. Today the State remains remote from every modern influence. It is an amazing, indeed a moving experience to a generation impatient of tradition and clamorous of progress. A world condemned perhaps, and for all that it loses nothing in poignancy.

She describes their visit to the island palace of Jagmandir:

We embarked at a little ghat in a backwater of the lake which, with a dramatic instinct perhaps accidental, gives no hint or promise of what is to come. It is not until five minutes later when you have been swept under a low white bridge, that the banks fall away and the splendour of the Palace and the lake is visible. The Children of the Sun must indeed reign here for a more beautiful light I have never seen than that which bathes these palaces, makes the trees glow as if cut out of emerald and throws shadows as blue as the deep sky on those white walls. Over the vast sweep of water, guarded by the hills, float these islands, each with its graceful Palace, each so lovely that detail escapes you in the wonder of the whole. The beauty of Mewar is the beauty of no other State I have seen. Not a single European silhouette, human or architectural. Far and near over the plain that leads to the village of Chitor and the foot of the great fortress, the Rajput horsemen sat erect and immoveable, sword in hand and shield slung to the shoulder, coloured cloths for saddles and streamers of scarlet and green and orange bound round their horses' heads. Chitor is to-day a centre of Hindu faith as it is the cradle of Hindu chivalry. The Sun is still worshipped in the temple built more than a thousand years ago, and every stone and every fragment on that scarred hillside is eloquent.

After a few days in the familiar atmosphere of dinner parties, lunches and meetings at Delhi to welcome the Lee Commission and guests from England, the Viceregal party set off south for Hyderabad and Mysore. They paused by the railway side for a dinner with the Maharajah of Datia.[7] Then they trundled on across the huge, arid, rock-studded plain of the Central Deccan and into the vast State of Hyderabad. No greater contrast to Rajasth'an could be imagined. His Exalted Highness the Nizam descended from one Mir Qamar-u-din Chin Qilich Khan whom the Emperor Aurangzebe appointed Viceroy of the Deccan: this man was of Persian origin and, as the Moghul Empire disintegrated, he turned his Viceroyalty into a kingdom. His descendants backed the British thus gaining the title of "Faithful Ally" and, by the twentieth century, Hyderabad had attained the position of premier State with the maximum revenue and salute of guns for the Ruler. An exclusively Muslim nobility, sophisticated, elegant, brilliant, ruled over a vast population of Hindus. Alice Reading, still suffering the after-effects of influenza, tackled the necessities of State:

On, on through the night to Hyderabad. We really had a splendid welcome but all I could do were the dullest functions. The State Banquet was in one of the Palaces, we sat down 300, everything was of gold, épergnes, vases, cruets, table cutlery, forks, spoons, even to the covers of the champagne bottles and the crumb scoop. His Exalted Highness the Nizam is an ugly little man with a horrible voice and worse temper. Everyone is terrified of him. One of his nobles arrived a minute after him, I hear it will cost him several lakhs. The stories that are told are too numerous and too lurid to repeat. He is worth millions and millions but Rumour says: "What he has, he holds and what everyone else has he holds as well, including their women folk." One of the nobles was going to send a magnificent motor car for my special use but none of the State officials would *guarantee* its *safe return*, so an ordinary Rolls-Royce was forthcoming instead. He was very amiable to us and to crown it all sent me a cheque for £2,000 the morning I left, saying he would keep my memory green! We were in a magnificent Palace all of marble, with a splendid collection of jade and crystal in the drawing room.

Her gossip about the Nizam had some truth in it. He was an eccentric man with different ideas of good and evil from the average Englishman. He also lacked the charm and sophistication of his long-suffering nobility, but there was something curiously kingly about that small, shabby figure, and a good brain flashed forth from behind his steel-rimmed spectacles.

The charm of Hyderabad could only be realised slowly. It was necessary to live there, to savour the good company and conversation, the total absence of any strain between British and Indians. The long days out among lakes and remote villages, shooting myriad snipe and duck, the majesty of Golconda and Daulatabad Forts, hewn out of living rock. There was a curious, often sinister glitter over all – as of ignis-fatuus on a bog. Little of this could reveal itself on a visit of three days.

A short pause in the garden paradise of Bangalore led on to Mysore. This state, so long in Muslim hands, was rendered back to a Hindu ruler in the nineteenth century. It was the scene of wars against Hyder Ali[8] and his son, Tipu, in which the future Duke of Wellington first showed his military quality. The state, after fifty years of British administration, became independent in 1881 and in Lord Reading's time was probably the best administered and most democratic in India. Poor Lady Reading! In the train from Bangalore to Mysore she passed a "hideous night" and had to stay behind and rest while the main party went out to the wonderful jungles. She writes on December 5th:

I have had to miss a lot through a gastric attack. I am going back to Bangalore for another 2 days rest and must leave the others to sight-see Trichinopoly, Madura and the Buddhist Temples. It is a great disappointment. Mysore was a wonderful sight, I have never seen such decorations and such crowds. They put up long festoons of glass drops here instead of paper decorations and at night huge transparencies on the archways with terrible coloured portraits of us both, double life size. The night we went to the Palace there were literally thousands and thousands of Indians in the big quadrangle in front of the Palace, about the size of the Place de la Concorde. The Maharajah[9] is charming, with such nice, quiet manners and wonderfully beloved by his people.

She describes fireworks and a torchlight procession, illuminated trick-riding and varieties of Indian music. On the way home the crowds were so great that police had to run each side of the car just to make room for its passage. At no time in the Reading Viceroyalty does there seem to have been such nervousness about safety as in, for instance, Lord Minto's day before World War I. Both the Viceroy and Lady Reading seem to have moved very freely among large crowds, often without any other protection than their Aides-de-camp on duty.

The highlight of the visit to Mysore was the *Keddah*, the trapping of wild elephants and their roping and securing by tame ones. It is a remarkably dangerous and skilful pitting of human wits against the jungle and Alice Reading was determined to see it.

Keddah Camp: A charming little red-roofed bungalow, just 2 bedrooms, bathroom and little sitting-room for H.E. and me, all round hundreds of tents. I got here, rested and then went to the Elephant Drive. This is the only place you can see this operation with wild elephants so I made up my mind I would go even if I had to crawl. I did not crawl, but was carried while H.E., the Maharajah and a few guests, trotted along the banks of a stream which was all surrounded by a tall fence with peep holes in it. We sat on *Austrian bent-wood chairs*, the others crouched. After about half-an-hour there was a terrific roar and an enormous elephant, the largest I have ever seen, came thundering down the opposite bank and took to the water, followed by about thirty others of all sizes and a yelling shouting mass of natives naked on a herd of tame elephants, with prongs, lighted torches and clappers making the most terrific and unearthly noises. I can only compare it to Dante's Inferno. The entire wild herd took to the water past where we were sitting, into a blockade of poles and bars and when they were all in, H.E. and I went on to a platform and he cut a rope whereby the hatchway fell down and all the beasts were safely housed.

It was a unique sight. The next day they were lassooed one by one, but I was not there having to take to my bed again. I forgot to say His Highness's wife and mother and all his female relations are in camp too and go each day from their bungalow to the Keddah where they have a Purdah tent. The mother is a remarkable woman, who through H.H.'s long minority did wonders for Mysore. The heir, a nephew, has a fascinating boy of 7 with a charming English nurse. He handed me a bouquet like a little courtier, gravely compared his jewellery with mine and when I left said, "You will come back again to Mysore, won't you?"

These are Yvonne's impressions:

There are, of course, wanton cruelties, and often you feel the beast to be so much finer than the man in his heart-broken struggle. All those months before the Keddah itself is reached, it is a fair fight between instinct and reasoned skill. Within the stockade it is barbarous, but it is no "show", but a huge organisation with a very definite purpose and use. The savage struggle is short and the pitiful thing to me is not so much the blood-stained heads and the queer pathetic cries but the baffled bewilderment of the wild. It is curious how vividly this huge, physical creature conveys the impression of mental agony.

Her Ex.'s next letter is dated December 13th:

We steamed punctually at 8 o'clock in the morning into Madras and I was delighted to see my dear Lord Willingdon.[10] It is so nice being here, except for fans very comfortable. The House is enormous and gorgeous with many treasures in the shape of old furniture, glass and china dating from John Company, with a lovely Ballroom built by Lord Clive.[11]

Yvonne's diary glows with enjoyment of beautiful eighteenth-century architecture in place of Victorian Gothic and the Public Works Department, the green, green gardens, the sea and (as Her Ex. also noticed) the smiling faces of the India that escaped invasion and the hand of conquest until the English came.

It was worth all my exertions to see the hundreds of smiling faces, each with two rows of perfect teeth. We never see a smile in North India. I loved it all, could not do otherwise. On my visit to the little Nuns at the top of St. Thomas's Mount,[12] I was carried by four gentlemen newly washed and dressed in white jerseys and scarlet knickers and blue cummerbunds, but I did not like the carrying process and only submitted to it as I cannot climb. The Nuns were sweet, so glad to talk French. All dressed in fine white Cashmere with ivory chains and crucifixes and their little faces looked as if carved in ivory too. They had, up till now, no water laid on and I had to turn it on for the first time amidst great rejoicing. I felt so guilty amidst all my luxury when I saw their empty spotless little rooms, with a bare floor and a little bed, a little pitcher of water! Still, my worldly soul rejoiced in a nice warm bath on my return.

Yvonne's final comment on Madras:

Madras seems to be less a city than a vast garden where houses happen. The two other Presidencies give themselves incredible airs, but compared with this Calcutta is pretentious and Bombay vulgar!

CHAPTER XIV

Burma and Baby Weeks

"These Burmese people . . . had still the pleasantness of their daily lives, their family loves, their coloured wear, their consciousness of superiority; the gay bubbles of their souls still flew against a painted sky in the golden glow of evening."

The Lacquer Lady by F. Tennyson Jesse

AS far back as June, 1923, Harcourt Butler noted: "I think the Viceroy may come to me at Christmas. I think this will save bickerings between them and the Lyttons at Calcutta." The Readings stayed with the Lyttons for a few days *en route* for Burma, as Belvedere was in the throes of redecoration. Her Ex.'s letters give no hint of bickerings:

I think this house splendid (we all admire one another's and not our own). They tell me it is inconvenient and dirty but it has magnificent reception rooms and marble corridors and represents something.

They were due to sail on a ship of the P. & O. fleet about which Harcourt Butler says: "Inchcape is going to turn the s.s. *Arankola* into a yacht for them. It is full of cockroaches. They recently cleared out 132 buckets without making much impression." Cockroaches are never mentioned by Lady Reading or Yvonne FitzRoy, so Lord Inchcape's minions must have done a good job. Yvonne says:

Perfect weather and a perfect ship which we shall all be terribly sorry to leave. We reach Rangoon at 3.30 to-day (December 21st, 1923), meanwhile here is a 5,000-ton vessel with ourselves as the only passengers, here are pheasants and salmon from Glenapp at extremely frequent intervals, here are State rooms in green for H.E., in mauve for Her Ex., and cabins in blue and gold for the rest of the company. Here too is incomparable sea, as flat as a pancake and as blue as the curtains.

Alice Reading fell in love with Burma and the Burmese, as many Europeans did in those days, coming from the infinitely more complex atmosphere of India, with all its taboos and suspicions. The English

Lady Reading arrives at Sir Hukum Chand's cotton mill, Indore
Lady Reading, Miss FitzRoy and Sister Meikle at Lakhota Fort, Jamnagar, with
H.H. the Jam Sahib Kumar Shri Ranjitsinhji

The Feast of Lanterns, Simla, September 1924. The Viceroy and Lady Reading with Megan Lloyd George are in the centre of the group, with Lady Erleigh kneeling in front
The Dragon who took part in the Chinese ballet at the Feast of Lanterns

connection with Burma was the result of undisguised military conquest, undertaken to safeguard the frontiers of the Indian Empire.[1] The Burmese have a very ancient homogeneous history and had, before the British expelled it, a picturesque royal house. There was little in Burma of inter-religious bitterness, no caste, and no purdah, for Burmese women have always been free to control their own property and have perfect liberty of movement. It may seem strange to have put the administration under the Government of India, but Indian Civil Service members who went there gave the country service, love and interest — which was not, however, returned in the same way. The Burmese never really accepted the British in their hearts; they went on their own way, often much more co-operative than Indians, but this was because it suited them to be so and because they are a merry people, not given to introspection and brooding. Harcourt Butler was twice at the head of the administration; the country suited his equable, gay and witty disposition, though he found European society boring and much enjoyed the stimulation of a Viceregal visit.

Megan Lloyd George[2] joined the party in Calcutta and Harcourt found her "a perfect dear. Not a bit spoilt, as keen as mustard, enjoys everything." Alice Reading writes:

December 24th. The morning of Christmas Eve! After an almost sleepless night through heat and mosquitoes I am trying to work myself up to a proper Christmas spirit, starting with the Hospital this morning and finishing up with a dinner and Investiture to-night. The place itself, with the exception of the Golden Pagoda [the Shwe Dagon] which dominates Rangoon, is a wee bit disappointing. You are not allowed in the sacred Pagoda, and with the exception of the Chain of Lakes there is not much sightseeing. The Lakes looked most lovely on the night of our arrival, the bamboos on either side being studded with coloured lights, and little ships all alight and gondolas sailing on the lakes. At the race course the crowd carried coloured umbrellas instead of the fascinating paper ones. The people came in their thousands to greet us. The men in bright coloured petticoats bunched in front, with pyjama-like jackets. The women adorable, skirts of every colour of the rainbow, tightly wound in the street and forming a long fan-shaped tail in the house. White linen pea-jackets, and their hair! At first I thought they were wearing high black satin caps, then discovered it was their own silky hair standing upright in a square and at the side, falling over their demure little faces, a bunch of what looked like white mimosa. The said cream coloured faces all chalked white, but so merry! All the crowd laughs at you, claps, waves and shows

9

such lovely teeth and dimples. I have lost my heart to the Rangoon people and wish I could take them back with me to India. On our drive to Government House (better known as St. Pancras Station, of which it is the facsimile) they piled up the bouquets all round me and then threw bunches of tuberoses into the carriage. On the 27th we leave for Mandalay which I believe is still more fascinating and not so European. Yesterday I made the Governor drive me through the Bazaars, such a feast of colour, all the men, women and babies in bright orange, pinks and blues.

Government House is very comfortable and has a magnificent Ballroom, the finest in India. The mosquitoes are a curse. I shall have to tell you more next week, tho' by then I expect we shall be steaming down the Irawaddy River, docsn't it sound alluring? I don't know what the steamers are like, but the Captain of the luxurious *Arankola* told me his ship was a second-class Boarding house in comparison to the Irawaddy Boat!

She was never able to make the comparison; the Burmese visit had to be cut short because of bad news from Afghanistan. There was trouble with the Afghan Government throughout 1923. Desperadoes from the tribal area, like the murderers of Mrs. Ellis and of Majors Orr and Anderson, took refuge in Afghanistan and could not be apprehended by the authorities in India. Relations with Afghanistan came under the Foreign Office which made the position difficult for the Viceroy. Lady Reading writes from the train running towards Delhi, January 2nd, 1924:

I can't remember if I described the Rangoon Garden party, with its dancing girls and boys playing "chilon", the national game? The "chilon" is a ball made of woven cane, the hands are not allowed to touch it, the ball is knocked to and fro by head, knee and toe. These boys did conjuring tricks, the like of which I have never seen, balancing glass balls on different parts of their body. They were hung with medals and the eldest boy, aged 11, when told to come up to H.E., advanced on his stomach with head touching the ground, hands raised in prayer. Next day, Mandalay. We had heard sad stories of rain spoiling the "Pandal" erected as a reception room, all painted yellow with pillars and coloured balls in the Burmese style. We had the reception in King Theebaw's old Palace where we were met by 8 gorgeous officials, all carrying Royal Umbrellas over us, made of creamed flounced Indian muslin, with stars of gold on them and gold sticks. The Audience Hall is all of gold. There are great teak pillars, all gilt and at one end Theebaw's throne, with gold doors behind through which he used suddenly to appear and look upon the crowd bowed down before him. I believe, on former occasions when Theebaw was alive, they had four men playing drums. The drums were hanging up and had white muslin petticoats round them, like the umbrellas. The Government House is fascinating – in fine weather. Next day, when it rained, I wished myself miles away. It is built of dark wood, Burmese fashion, all open and one side an old wall literally leans up against the House, with a large Moat all round. The Burmese love the water and are splendid rowers, men and women. The women rowing often with great cheroots in their mouths! Before the Regatta next day there was an entertainment given us by the town of Mandalay, in the Old Palace Gardens at night. The people came in thousands and were allowed everywhere so that with the exception of a few Police officers and our Aides we mingled freely with a cheering, excited crowd. Their dancing consists almost entirely of bending about the body into extraordinary positions. The movement most admired is made with the arm, bending the elbow the wrong way. They have tiny arms and hands and twist them and their little fingers all the time.

We had to give up our trip on the Irawaddy, and to the Burma oil fields. The Regatta was the most picturesque entertainment we have ever had. Men and women in all their brightest colours thronged the banks of the Moat. It was a wonderful scene when we embarked on a marvellous barge, the boat accompanying us on either side filled with men and women of Mandalay who kept up a continuous chant. The crowds all along the banks gave us a rousing reception, there was a riot of colour, and so ended our stay with the hospitable people of Burma.

Note from Harcourt Butler, tired but satisfied, in spite of the rain and the curtailed visit: "The Viceroy and Lady R. have both mellowed into their position as all Viceroys do, and expect more. But they have not changed to me. It is a treat talking to the Viceroy, he is so quick and his outlook is so different. I like Mr. Harry Isaacs [Lord Reading's brother]. He says he has not felt at home anywhere except in my house. He can't stand all the bowing and scraping!" A Viceroy has no honour in his own family.

Back in Delhi, the usual programme went on its way. There was some novelty in the Legislative Assembly as the Swarajist Party were:

. . . well to the fore, and for the first time the benches will be filled with men in Khaddar [home-spun cloth]. I have been giving days to Baby Week and visitors. Monday, I visited the Baby Show, all the various exhibits, and spoke to the workers, finishing up with the cinema play which was a present to me from 6 leading Calcutta men: "Save the Babies". Very well done, this will be given twice a day all the week. Tuesday was the official opening and H.E. and I drove in State to the ground where the

Committee of 45 awaited us. After 2 short speeches from H.E. and the Delhi Commissioner, I spoke and people were very nice about it. It was a huge audience, including the Commander-in-Chief and many soldiers, H.E.'s Council and members of the Legislative Assembly. The whole thing has caught on most tremendously. Although I have asked for no money I am constantly receiving cheques and, what is still better, requests that it should be an annual affair. From far away Kathiawar I had a letter from the one Englishwoman (a doctor) saying the Ruling Prince loved children, they had a wonderful Baby Week and H.H. wanted to hold it every year. Madras Municipal Council passed a vote requesting the Government to open a Fund to erect a statue of me and a plaque in every Infant Welfare Centre "to one who loved Indian children". I tell you all this (it sounds horribly conceited!) but I know it interests you. Tomorrow I go again by special request of the women, it is "Purdah" day, and will talk to them through an interpreter, and Saturday I go to judge the babies.

Harcourt Butler had great fun with his Baby Week in Rangoon:

21st March: I have been very busy with Baby Week. This is Lady Reading's movement. It is a good movement. One child in three dies in infancy here. The Baby Week was run by Burmans and really was a great success. There was some real enthusiasm and things were done in the way the people like. That is what we have got to work for. One of the features was a street, on one side VIRTUE and on the other VICE. It was run by medical students and was very amusing. I must admit that the vicious side of the street attracted the mass of the spectators. The book-makers, the gambling hell, the dancing saloon and the opium den were more amusing than the reading club, the forge, etc.!

It is pleasant to remember Alice Reading surging through the crowds on Purdah Day for she really loved them. From all accounts it would seem that rich babies won the best medals, but especial arrangements were made for poor babies to get something too, and there was a good deal of handing on of the tickets issued to prize-winners, so that the same medal could be applied for more than once. The Girl Guides worked hard, cleaving a way for Her Ex. through the throng and though some may mock at the whole idea as paternalistic and futile, it was human, friendly and spontaneous, sowing the seeds for further good work of a more professional nature. In addition to the films called "Save the Babies" and "The Cry of the Children", there was also a film on Child Marriage, presented by Rabindranath Tagore.[3]

On January 12th, Mr. Gandhi, still in prison, underwent an operation for appendicitis and as soon as it became known agitation arose for his release. Although the extremist members of the Assembly still showed their unwillingness to meet the Viceroy halfway, the political situation had stabilised and this was therefore an unwelcome development—a choice between making a martyr of Mr. Gandhi or yielding to popular agitation. However, it was also clear that once Mr. Gandhi regained his freedom he would use it primarily in battle with his fellow Swarajists to prevent them co-operating with the government by entering the Legislature, and that while he was busy with this he would not become a threat to law and order. Gandhi was not yet the Mahatma, and his release did not make very much stir. His time was still to come.

In a letter dated February 13th, Alice Reading mentions, for the first time, Mahommed Ali Jinnah,[4] the founder of Pakistan. (He had had private interviews with the Viceroy before this.) In those days he was the leader of the "Independent" Party in the Assembly and an object of interest more because of his startlingly beautiful wife than for any other reason.

Most of our guests are spending their mornings at the Legislative Assembly where the Swarajist members are causing some excitement. One of the latest recruits to the Legis. Assembly is a young lawyer from Bombay called Jinnah. I did not hear him speak but popular opinion says he is an Indian Lloyd George. He came to lunch with his wife. Very pretty, a "complete minx" . . . She is a Parsee and he a Mahommedan. [Their marriage convulsed both communities.] She had less on in the day time than anyone I have ever seen. A tight dress of brocade cut to waist back and front, no sleeves, and over it and her head flowered chiffon as a sari. Mostyn-Owen, one of our Aides, who is rather a good young man, said to her that the hotel where she is living as "nice and quiet at night", to which she replied, "I don't like nice, quiet nights, I like a lot going on!"

Mrs. Jinnah's dress or lack of it would invoke no comment to-day, but in 1924 her beautiful golden midriff caused a considerable sensation, especially in the gallery at the Assembly where she was to be seen every day. Yvonne describes her saris as "economical in function".

The rest of the cold weather season proved to be hectic. The Lee Commission was in session all the time working out better conditions of pay and leave for the Services. Innumerable visitors came and went, British and American, and every now and then the Viceroy and some of his guests made a dash to some nearby Maharajah—Alwar, Bharatpur,

Dholpur[5]— to shoot some bird or beast. Lord Reading's tigers and panthers were furiously and earnestly discussed in British society and also in the pages of *The Field*. Alice Reading is impatient, in her letters, with guests who did not play bridge, as she then had to play Mah Jong with them—

> . . . which I do not understand, so cordially dislike. Sometimes I rebel and we play "Rummy" after dinner, a hand of glorified Poker only less of a gamble.

Balls, Investitures, receptions, Polo, Horse Show followed the accustomed pattern. Alice Reading is noticeably less excited about these functions than she had been to begin with. Details are not given in such profusion, and a certain weariness is more obvious. But she can still rise to an Infant Welfare Centre:

> Tuesday. Infant Welfare Centres. Hundreds of babies with remnants of shirts, and that was all. They received the sweeties I brought them in a scrap of their rags, the mothers pressed round me, stroked my skirts and uttered prayers, all starting: "Oh, my Mother . . ." I do love helping them, they are such poor neglected people. My Miss Griffin and Miss Graham are priceless assets. I am sure they ought to have a front seat in the Kingdom of Heaven! Meanwhile I am sending them home on holiday.
> Bodyguard Sports yesterday in celebration of the 150th Anniversary of the Bodyguard—Warren Hastings, 1774, Earl of Reading, 1924. All the splendid Veterans from Allahabad, Lucknow, Lahore, etc., came to join in. We gave them a supper at night and distributed prizes of watches and warm clothes. At night the Masonic Ball, everyone dressed up in scarlet, pale blue, dark blue silk aprons, decorations. Such a funny show, but such a good thing as one of the few where English and Indians unite. The Masons gave me a pair of long white gloves on a white suède cushion, trimmed with pale blue, as a token.

The Governor-General's Bodyguard was recruited from Indian cavalry regiments with a strength part Sikh and part Punjaubi Mussulman. The men had to be over six feet in height and of fine record. Mounted mostly on thoroughbred English and Australian horses of a size equal to the riders, they were a splendid sight and the uniform far more brilliant and colourful than the Lifeguards or the Blues. The tie of the Punjaubi *pagri* and the netted beards of the enormous Sikhs were particularly striking.[6] The Presidency Governors, Calcutta, Madras and Bombay, had smaller but similar household cavalry. The

Governor-General's men had their permanent headquarters at Dehra Dun where they kept a large farm for horse-fodder, and vegetables for their families who lived there.

Alice Reading did not take kindly to Lord Leverhulme[7] who was "doing" Delhi in three days:

> As he was not using his usual ear trumpet I had to roar all my remarks into his ear and was utterly exhausted by the end of lunch. He is a tiny, foxy-looking little man and amused me very much by his description of the Augustus John portrait of him. He obviously did not think the great A.J. did him justice for he informed me Laszlo had painted a beautiful portrait of him in Peer's robes with which he was *quite in love*, and proceeded to take a photo of it from his pocket book and exhibit it!

One wonders if Her Ex. used *her* ear-trumpet on this occasion; if not, it must have been a case of mutual roaring.

> March 12. We are sitting here puffing and blowing with all the electric fans on. We have still a full house, among others the Boltons[8] who have taken Sir John Maffey's place in Peshawar. Also Colonel Humphreys[9] from Kabul. He is very funny about Afghanistan. It seems he faithfully promised the Amir he should have an heir, fortunately a boy did appear else I tremble for his head.
>
> There is great excitement about the Legislative Assembly, after throwing out several Bills they are calming down. One man got up and said what had we, the Europeans, done for India? We had brought influenza! On 28th I go to Dehra Dun. I had meant to vegetate but I hear they are taking "advantage of my presence" to hold a Baby Week, it follows me wherever I go.
>
> This is written at 7 at night, but it is so hot that I am holding my pen with difficulty and my brain refuses to work. I have had a wearying day arranging all about the Opening Ceremony of my Hospital, April 25th, also a Committee on Baby Week for next year.

On April 1st the Viceroy went off to the Central Provinces, the finest jungle area in India. After the various ceremonies, inspections and interviews required of him, he disappeared into the forests and shot seven tigers, a not unusual number in that part of India where they were a positive menace to the aboriginal tribes who treated them rather like rabbits and were known to club them off cattle with little axes. It was much appreciated if anyone came along to reduce the tiger population. Her Ex. went alone to Dehra Dun which she found:

. . . beautifully cool, some welcome showers. The bungalow has been re-thatched, looks very attractive, the hollyhocks reach the thatch and the orange tree outside my door has lovely yellow fruit and a mass of blossom which smells very weddingy. The Staff take it in turns to go into the jungle to see the tigers come at 5 a.m. to drink at the pools but so far have only seen two panthers. Megan is very keen on the jungle, I only regret that it is such rough going I cannot attempt it. One of the Aides came home wildly excited yesterday as he had shot a Python, it was asleep under a tree having gorged a small deer. The skin makes splendid shoes, they never wear out. It is most interesting watching and studying the habits of the wild animals. You will be amused when I tell you my literature when I lunch alone is *The Life of the Scorpion*.

The Willingdons leave this week for home, they will be greatly missed. She has the most marvellous vitality and energy of any woman I have ever met. He is a very perfect gentleman and most popular. We are watching affairs at home with great interest, the continual defeat of the Government does not look well. Here we have a little pause as the Legislative Assembly does not sit again till May. It is true Gandhi has summoned his principal followers to Bombay and all sorts of rumours are afloat; to me it seems such an impasse, that it is difficult to see the way out. Meanwhile H.E. is having a delightful holiday which makes me very happy. We start on our fourth year; next year will mean going up to Simla for the last time!

CHAPTER XV

The Fourth Round

"Chinga-Ringa-Ring-Tum! Feast of Lanterns,
Horra-Korra-Chop-Sticks, Songs and Gongs!"

Nursery Rhyme

AS soon as Her Ex. reached Simla on April 15th she visited her hospital which was to be opened on the 25th:

My room is full of flowers, iris, mauve orchids, wisteria and great vases of pale yellow Banksia roses. It is wonderful having five gardens a year. After leaving Delhi all withered and finished meeting fresh, young green and herbaceous border at Dehra Dun and then coming here and starting anew. This morning, flanked by Doctor and Sister, went off to see my hospital. I am very pleased indeed with it, it really is a lovely site and they have made a good job of it. The Women's large Ward has turned out splendidly with long windows to the verandah where we can wheel the beds out, the view heavenly. The Children's Ward is charming, with tiled walls and pale green india rubber floor, and cupboards in walls with glass doors for toys I have bought them.

It was so nice coming back here yesterday, every man, woman and child came out of their shops and houses to bid me welcome.

Yvonne FitzRoy truly remarks at one point in her diary, "Simla is not India". It was a creation of the British and the Indian population not seriously politically conscious. This may be why Alice Reading felt at home there, because she was essentially a personal character and found it hard to understand why everyone could not live together in peace and harmony since her intentions were benign, therefore so must those of others be also. She prepared her hospital as for English women and children; it never occurred to her that people of lower standards of living could do with less. It did worry her later that patients wandered into the garden and climbed back on the clean white beds with muddy feet, and that the families of patients camped under and around their sick. She writes most endearingly about the toys provided for the children, as the wards filled up throughout the summer noting that she had never seen Indian children *play* before and that they loved the dolls and "woolly bears". She shopped busily searching for furniture for the enormous Doll's House which stood in the ward, and was distressed because the Doctor-in-charge begged her not to go to the expense of providing a small brass flower vase for each bedside locker as these would inevitably disappear when the cured patients returned home.

The opening proved a tremendous success; even the weather was perfect as a spring day in the Himalayas can be:

> H.E. and I drove with full Bodyguard to the Mall where we were met by the Building Committee. We then drove in rickshaws to where a big Arch announced "The Lady Reading Hospital for Women and Children". All the paths were lined by Boy Scouts and Girl Guides and we went in procession to the dais. H.E. spoke, I spoke, Sir Mahommed Shafi spoke with great emotion and Mr. Montagu Butler presented me with a gold key and I unlocked the main doors and flung them open. The sun shone, the birds sang, the garden was full of pansies and lupins, wallflowers and stocks, so peaceful, as if no sickness or death could find a place. The Nurses were there in each ward, all the Hospital Staff in new liveries. By the way, thereby hangs a tale. I was at the Hospital in the morning until 1 o'clock and we opened at 5.30. At the last minute I had not seen the liveries which I had designed. Dark blue, with golden yellow vests and turbans, and leather bands with brass buckles. When a man tried one of these on it looked hideous, he looked like a trussed guinea pig. I had it all taken to pieces and I left disconsolate as in three rooms there were no curtains, six screens had not been covered, altogether behindhand. By 5.30 the man met me at the door in *full fig*, four others behind him. All four liveries had been finished in time, all curtains were made up, each Ward had its screens!! This is to show you what they can do with only two men crouched on the floor with sewing machines, one to cut and one to fit. On Monday 34 patients arrive, this at once shows you how futile the comments are, "Indian women will not go to hospital".
>
> Two days ago Colonel Carey-Evans[1] left us amidst weeping and wailing. He was just as miserable at going as we all were at his departure.

"Carey", as everyone called him, had been Her Ex.'s strength and stay in every way from the first. Not only as a skilful and considerate physician, but as chief administrator in her hospital and welfare work. His wife, Lloyd George's eldest daughter Olwen, had gone home with their children in the winter and he now followed them. He was succeeded by Colonel Norman-Walker, also a great help to Her Ex. who reported with relish that Mrs. Norman-Walker "is reputed to be one of the world's *workers*". She missed the help of wives on the staff. The new Private Secretary, Geoffrey de Montmorency,[2] the Comptroller, "Smiler" Muir,[3] and the Military Secretary, Colonel Worgan,[4] were all bachelors. Wives on a Viceregal or Government House Staff acted as extra A.D.C.s (unpaid) and could be invaluable if they had any gift for public work.

Megan Lloyd George shone in the firmament of Simla that season. She seemed determined to make up for a girlhood of fascinating, but very adult, political life, by entering enthusiastically into every activity. She had a sweet voice, a great talent for acting and a most joyous, simple, unspoilt heart.

With the new hospital launched, Her Ex. turned her attention to the grim old one and decided to adapt it for health teachers' and mid-wives' training:

> I have cajoled some money out of the Municipality and am trying to get them to build a lecture room and quarters for midwives.

She notes an interesting social development, the first sign of a new dispensation in India which was to sever by degrees the ties that bound the British to the land in which they worked:

> Simla has altered a lot, or rather its population. So many people are away on leave, they tell me over 150 houses are empty this season. Formerly all the wives came up here from the Plains in the hot weather, but now they mostly go home for the children's summer holidays.

The Lee Commission Passages—that is assistance with the cost of fares home, altered the habits of the British considerably even before air transport gave the final blow to hill stations. But in spite of reduced numbers, this was the gayest season ever. Alice Reading's talent for entertaining and her original ideas seemed to inspire others to emulate her. The Black Heart Fancy Dress Revel broke all records, with a special Cotillion, favours from Paris and the most beautiful young married woman in Simla as Queen of the Revels. In those days girls did not take pride of place, except in the top set of State Lancers, with the Viceroy as the chief among the dancers. The Simla Amateur Dramatic Society also excelled itself that year. It was an old-established society dating from 1887 and performances took place in a tiny theatre belonging to the Municipality. It had been very well designed and must once have resembled one of those pretty play-houses built for their pleasure by German Grand Dukes. It had a tier of boxes like Covent Garden, with the State Box in the middle, stalls and two galleries. The stage was large and well-planned, but over the years everything became dirtier and more decayed and the dressing-rooms tested the nerves even of the most ardent player, since the walls were full of bugs and the grime of ages plastered the floor. However, great was the glamour of a final curtain after a run of five evening performances and two matinées. All the women eyed each other's pile of bouquets jealously, since far more than stage proficiency dictated the number and size of the tributes. Hearts were broken and mended again on that stage and many riotous parties took place on it and in the Green Room. The V.I.P.s of Simla and their staffs always attended the performances and a special note of congratulation from any of them gave great pleasure and afforded much kudos. That summer the Society gave *The Private Secretary*, *Ambrose Applejohn's Adventure*, *The Dover Road*, and *Dear Brutus*. The musical (there was always one every season), was *Tonight's The Night*, in which Megan played a big part. The "*clou*", as Her Ex. would say, was an Apache dance in which the future Member for Carmarthen was swung wildly round the stage on a strong leather belt, wielded by a muscular and handsome Captain of Artillery. The permanent stage manager who had been there, it seemed, from the beginning of time, was called Mr. de la Rue Brown, almost the dirtiest thing in the theatre. Everyone accepted him as part of the fittings and in the midst of chaos he went about with a chewed cheroot in his mouth yelling and cursing at the unfortunate Indians who pulled curtains and worked the lights. "It will be all right on the night," he used to say, and it always was.

The greatest party of all that year was Lady Reading's Feast of Lanterns. Anyone present at it will always remember it as a party to beat all parties. Lady Reading organised this Feast towards the end of the season to welcome her son and daughter-in-law, Lord and Lady Erleigh. This is how she herself tells of it:

> September 4th. The Chinese Ball has overshadowed everything else, it really was a great show. The House looked wonderful, the Hall, Ballroom and Dining-room covered in Chinese panels and thousands of lanterns. The Ballroom scheme all scarlet, the dining room orange and the Hall bright blue. The Hall was dimly lit and as you came in you were met by nodding Chinamen, the entire Staff dressed in black satin jackets and

bright blue satin trousers, felt shoes, satin caps with pigtails, made up with slanting eyebrows and eyes and drooping moustaches till they were unrecognizable. We had a very cheery dinner first, all the girls who acted, about 20, came in to dinner with the Staff and made up a large party. At 9.30 we were conducted to a Chinese Pagoda on the stage where the Band usually sit. They were relegated to an alcove made up Chinese fashion in red enamel and they all wore Chinese dress. The dresses of the guests were lovely, some priceless old Chinese coats amongst them. About 350 guests greeted us Chinese fashion, the men prostrating themselves, the women bowing with folded arms, turning their heads from one side to the other, and stroking their knees. A fanfare of trumpets and then to Chinese music[5] 20 of Simla's prettiest girls danced charmingly. Then the lights went out and they each had a scarlet electric torch and danced in and out. A gong sounded, and through bright blue curtains emerged an enormous Dragon, about 7 feet long, with motor lamp eyes, a marvellous creation made by Mr. Bertram, our Estate carpenter. Out of the Dragon came Miss Lyndall (the pretty Spanish looking girl who teaches dancing). She was dressed all in white and gold and did a marvellous Chinese dance, sinking down at the end cross-legged at our feet. The doors opened again and a procession of girls dressed as water carriers with pails of red, blue and orange sunshades I had sent from Burma, a sunshade for every man and a sandal wood fan for every woman. One more figure—Megan in a charming Burmese costume in a Chinese rickshaw with Miss FitzRoy and Miss Worgan back and front of the rickshaw dressed as Coolies. Megan salaamed and presented H.E. with a gold sunshade and me with a gold fan wrapped in purple silk, in true Burmese style. Then everyone, unfurling fan and unfolding sunshade, started dancing, it was really a lovely sight. At supper the tables were all in Chinese colours with birds' nests (made of chocolate) and chopsticks complete.

Her Ex. does not describe the dresses in detail, leaving this to Yvonne:

Patiala had risen magnificently to the occasion and, as a warlike Samurai of some remote date, with leather coat steel embossed, and gold and steel helmet, was quite the most striking figure in the room. Both Sir Narasimha Sarma and Mr. Chatterjee[6] deserve full credit. For "dressing up" is surely a purely British form of lunacy.

It would seem almost as if Alice Reading heard Time's winged chariot, for she did not waste one minute of this summer and it turned out to be the last full season for her in Simla. She visited her hospital twice a week and is full of stories of it:

Yesterday I visited my Hospital with a party of Purdah ladies who could not view it at the general opening. Over 30 patients had arrived the day before from the old Dufferin Hospital and we are anxiously awaiting the birth of the first baby, who will get a silver rattle from me. It is a race between two, great excitement prevails. The Medical Ward is nearly full, several in Children's Ward. This morning I had a funny, froggy little man from the Municipality who came to thank me in the name of his countrymen and to tell me how delighted the Bazaar people are.

June 6th. This has been a breathless week with "Royal" birthdays, Investiture, dinner and reception. We went Friday to Mashobra with 10 of the Staff and 12 more people, including 4 friends rode out to lunch and picnic tea for *my* birthday. I thought we would be nice and quiet out there, eight miles away, but 7.30 in the morning the first basket of flowers arrived and at 11 at night the last cable and letter of congratulations.

In addition to congratulations on her birthday, Lady Reading received them for the award of the Kaisar-i-Hind medal which the King bestowed upon her in the Birthday Honours. Maharajahs Bharatpur and Patiala vied in bringing amazing birthday cakes to The Retreat. The Bharatpur one had a model of her little Austin car on the top, because he had lent it to her. The Patiala cake carried the Star of India and His Highness' coat-of-arms, and gold steps (sugar) leading to a marzipan throne. The members of the Legislative Assembly followed up with a cake decorated with a model of the new hospital.

Everyone showered me with presents, from a lovely book-plate to a toy elephant. I came home laden on Monday morning after a wonderful picnic in the woods.

This picnic started very formally, with everyone curtseying round the table-cloth laid on the greensward, but it ended in a rag, Her Ex. throwing apricots as vigorously as anyone.

On June 12th Lady Reading records with interest two mixed marriages between Mr. Chatterjee, a Member of Council, and a Miss Broughton, and another between a Parsee, Mr. Sorabji, and a Miss Monkhouse. At the time these marriages caused immense discussion and some shock among both British and Indians. Alice Reading takes it all very calmly, is interested but wonders about possible children and their future. Talking of children, she goes on to describe the green and white striped pyjamas the children wear in her hospital, "they look ducks in them". There must have been some surprise on the part of both children and mothers, since most Indian babies of the poorer class do not wear anything below the waist until they are old enough to keep clean without supervision.

I did not tell you of our trouble with smallpox, we got a woman in hospital who developed it. Entire hospital and Staff had to be vaccinated and so had I as I had gone the day before right up to her bed, but had not touched her. Usually they hold my hand or stroke my dress or pat me, but she looked rather red so I kept aloof. Now all is well, no fear of infection. I have collected now just on £100,000 sterling in three years, but you need some driving power to see it through. Between 60 and 70 patients now. People are coming from far and wide, if only I had built it twice the size.

Lady Elizabeth Matheson is staying with us (she is Lord Albemarle's daughter, only married six months) and at a dinner last night old Lady Shafi lent forward confidentially and said in a stage whisper, "How many little ones have you got?" Captain Mostyn-Owen, who always blurts everything out (he is a great dear) assured me that Lady Helen Barlow, who had fainted and been taken out, "was all right lying on the sofa outside with Colonel Norman-Walker." This is the lighter side of life! Politically things are quite lively, Bengal particularly. The Chief of Police from there has been on a visit, I feel sorry for his poor wife as he is permanently shadowed and travels under an assumed name as he has enemies.

I have to confess that H.E. and I have fallen victims and this last week have had four dancing lessons from a fascinating female. If you saw H.E. and me solemnly prancing down the huge ballroom to a foxtrot on the gramophone you would smile—as I do. To-day we are sufficiently advanced to dance to a small jazz band.

A good story about an unusual patient at the hospital:

We have one poor woman there who was found in the backwoods with a gangrened foot, of which we have had to relieve her. She speaks no known language and is said to be a "Bear Woman", that is a woman brought up by bears. There are such here in the wilds. This story has got about and Indians come in dozens to view her. She is out on the verandah and the last I saw of her she was crawling on all fours because of the loss of her foot, but the Indians say because she was taught this by the bears. All day long even our own servants are asking for passes to go and "view" her. I am furious, but it is impossible to convince them that they must leave her alone.

Lord Lytton came up from Bengal to discuss a very troubled situation there. The Viceroy had been reluctantly compelled to re-introduce Regulation 111 of 1818, an old enactment of the East India Company

which was revived from time to time to enable Government to deal
with violent revolutionary crime. It empowered the authorities to
order arrest and detention at will. Murders and outrages by *dacoits*
(robber gangs) against Indian and British people in Bengal in 1923–4
made the Regulation necessary. However, its enactment was much
criticised by the Labour Government then in power in Britain and it
was used as an excuse for the Swarajists in the Bengal Council to
accentuate wrecking tactics. Lord Lytton and the Viceroy also had a
difference of opinion to smooth over with regard to a reading of the
Government of India Act of 1919. Their personalities were not
sympathetic one to another, but on this visit to Simla they came to an
understanding and achieved a stronger mutual personal regard. Alice
Reading found Lord Lytton—

> . . . every day more like his Father and Grandfather, minus the beard,
> and he is a very well informed person, only has rather a pedagogic manner.
> He has a very difficult job in Bengal. Things are not easy out here and
> never will be. Delhi has been misbehaving itself, and most of the deaths
> and bloodshed caused by people telling lies and thus fostering ill-feeling.
> Even when I held my Baby Week in Delhi some wretched people went
> about trying to spread propaganda that I wanted to get hold of all the
> babies to Christen them. Just my line!!

Mr. and Mrs. Jinnah came to dinner in September—

> . . . she with less clothes and more golden brown skin showing than I have
> ever seen before. Her attire was a Liberty scarf, a jewelled bandeau and an
> emerald necklace! She ran away to marry him and is now an outlaw from
> her race much to her own amusement. She is extremely pretty, fascinating,
> terribly made up. All the men raved about her, the women sniffed!
>
> Gerald and Eva [Erleigh] sail on Saturday by the *Macedonia*, the only
> fly in the ointment being that they had to give up their Khyber Pass trip.
> There is such unrest there that H.E. did not care for them to take a pleasure
> trip in those regions. Things have been horrid up there, the old story of
> religious friction. The Hindu-Moslem question is one of the most difficult
> H.E. has to tackle. I forgot to tell you about the reception we gave
> to members of the Legislative Assembly. There were hundreds there
> including Pandit Malavya in his home-spun. He was very flattering about
> my hospital and work and strongly urged me not to go in a year-and-a-half's
> time but to stay indefinitely! He is on his way to Gandhi who has started
> a 21-day fast, only taking water and salt, as a protest against the Hindu-
> Muslim atrocities at Kohat. I do feel sorry for Gandhi, I do believe he is
> sincere. He is terribly delicate and looks skin and bone and so transparent.

At the end of September a most terrible storm broke over Simla. The monsoon proper had ceased, followed by the usual spell of exquisite diamond weather. The Erleighs started off down the hill and mercifully got as far as the main line before the "roaring hillside broke":

> There never was such a storm. We are cut off from beyond Simla. I do not even know how our food gets up. Tonight we were to have had our final "At Home" for 400 people, all put off because no electric light. Terrible rumours of landslides reach us hourly. The latest is that Patiala was out motoring and is a fixture as the cliff has landslipped behind him and in front of him.

In time the storm passed and presumably the Maharajah was rescued, the numerous trains cooped up (like the Maharajah) at the junction half-way down the hill managed to move again and wonderful weather returned.

> This is my last letter from my beloved Simla. It is like Spring in Switzerland, the narcissi all out, men coming in from the woods selling great bundles. The snows are a joy each morning and evening. In six days' time we leave for Kashmir. Fortunately there are no State functions, we stay at the nice Residency. H.E. goes up in the mountains shooting most of the time, so Megan, Miss F., Sister and I and two Aides will go picnicking. Simla was terribly knocked about by the gale and some hair-breadth escapes as there were 77 landslides in Simla alone and one bridge after another went on the railway. Our little toy train did not come up at all and lots of people we know were four days doing one night's journey.
>
> We are all looking forward to Kashmir, though the six months at Simla have slipped away so quickly.

10

CHAPTER XVI

Cashmere, Cattis and Caves

"Mante to deo nahin to bhit ka leo—If you believe, it is a God. If not, plaster detached from a wall."

Indian Proverb

KASHMIR in 1921 had been Alice Reading's first experience of a State visit and she had looked upon it with wondering eyes. The undertones of discontent and intrigue and even the pouring rain had not damped her enthusiasm. Now in the autumn of 1924 her reactions were different. Satiated with ceremony she accepted bizarre episodes as a matter of course, and turned her eyes to scenery.

For the last three weeks of the hectic Simla season she had been far from well. In fact her first appearance at dinner was for the Viceroy's birthday party on October 10th. They were all tired, even Yvonne's diary sounds a jaded note. The one exception was the Viceroy himself. Bronzed and lively after a short shooting trip in the Hills, he gave the impression, says his wife, of being 44 rather than 64. Next day "that torturing journey down the hill", as Yvonne puts it, writing at Domel, their first night stop on the way to Kashmir:

> We may be forgiven for feeling a trifle dazed for did we not breakfast yesterday at 7,500 feet, dine at 500, breakfast this morning at 1,000, have luncheon at 6,000 and now propose sleeping at 2,000. We covered the best part of 90 miles by road to-day, travel 40 to Uri tomorrow and finish the trail to Srinagar on Tuesday. Domel is looking very pretty and we dined on the verandah. About a mile up the road we saw four men crossing the Jhelum on *mussacks* — an inflated goat-skin — which serves to keep them afloat while they propel and guide themselves by feet and hands.

Lady Reading takes up the tale:

> October 13th. We are comfortably settled at Uri for one night only. H.E. and I are using my Cadillac which, in spite of Rolls-Royces, remains my favourite car. It is a tremendously winding road, needing very careful driving with horrid little bridges we have to cross continuously over little mountain torrents. We leave again at 9 tomorrow, halt at 1 for lunch, rest

and change clothes then meet the Maharajah and go up the Jhelum River, as two years ago. I am feeling better but not right yet; now 8 o'clock, am just going to bed to get all the rest I can. I can see the stars come out and all the bustle of camp life from where I lie as only bead curtains in the doorway. If anyone had told me 4 years ago that I should go to bed like this!! I have been sprinkling Keatings over my bed, carpets, etc., as there are many unwelcome visitors besides mosquitoes, but life is wonderful and unless I am really ill I enjoy every moment of it.

She does not mention that there was a considerable earth tremor during the night before when they halted at Shalting, and her next letter from Srinagar is ecstatic:

The Residency, Srinagar. October 18th. Here we are at our old spot, only so much more beautiful than three years ago at the same time of year; then it was cold and wet and all leaves turned brown. Now it is the most perfect spring weather with just a cold nip in the air, dew on the grass in the early morning. At Shalting was Sir Hari Singh,[1] the heir, on crutches — he has broken his leg in two places tobogganing a few months ago so could not accompany us. The little Maharajah was on the quay to welcome us, and was most dissatisfied with my looks (I was terribly tired) and whenever anyone said, "Her Ex. looks well," he said, "No! No!" and shook his head. We went up the river on a steam launch as it is an unofficial visit. We were hailed with joy by many old friends at Schools, Nursing Homes and Hospitals en route. We had a most tremendous reception passing the Muslim Mosque. They turned out in their thousands to cheer H.E. who fought their battles. The Maharajah is a Hindu and he glanced at H.E. out of half-closed eyes, little escapes him.

On Thursday we had a Garden Party at the Nishat Bagh. I hope to be able to send you a snapshot of the Maharajah between H.E. and me with a hand in each of ours. The garden looked exquisite. I have never seen such zinnias or salvias, all the thousands of fountains playing and on each step a Royal Red soldier or Police. 4 terribly smart gentlemen dressed like Corsicans in scarlet and gold carried me up one flight of steps after the other. The next day we lunched at Shalimar Bagh, the other beautiful garden, a party of almost forty, outside on a black marble verandah this time, all fountains playing, also the Maharajah's band, also a Piper playing Scotch tunes, walking up and down by the fountains, rather incongruous. It is so lovely here, air like champagne, such sunshine and blue skies, I feel better already.

The two gardens were laid out by Jehangir in the seventeenth century with all the Moghul genius for such work. Kashmir was under

Muslim rule from 1339 onwards until conquered by the Sikh Ranjit
Singh in the nineteenth century. After the defeat of the Sikhs the
British sold the Vale of Kashmir to a Dogra noble called Golab Singh,
from whom the ruler who welcomed the Readings descended. Dogras
are Rajputs who left their native land before the Mahommedan invasion
of it, to carve out small principalities for themselves from the hill
tracts round Kangra and Jammu. Thus Dogras can claim never to have
been conquered by Islam, but when one of their race became master
over Kashmir he ruled a predominantly Muslim population, a situation
giving rise to immense problems ever since.

Yvonne's diary tells of a visit to Gulmarg further up into the mountains, and bird and bear shoots. Lady Reading took part in none of
these and as this is her story, they must remain unrecorded. She
writes on October 25th:

Our lovely stay here is, alas! drawing to a close. We have been to the
"Serai" here to-day and I took four American ladies with me, relatives
of a friend of mine; they were armed with Kodaks and their joy knew no
bounds. It certainly is a wonderful sight, like a huge market with mules
laden with merchandise and all round men of every nationality all more
or less wild-looking. I sat on the only chair, covered with some of the
white felt "numdahs" (or mats) they sell here. At my feet ghastly carpets
with lions and tigers printed on in the vilest dyes, and then the men came
and laid at my feet, in a dirty handkerchief, Turquoise Matrix, bits of
Kashmerian jade, bright coloured silks and handkerchiefs, jade and ivory
bangles. All the American women went off delighted with souvenirs.
Yesterday the Maharani welcomed me in the lovely Shalimar Gardens.
She had been studying English and understood a bit of what I said. She
looked so attractive in a wonderful tent made of crimson and gold embroidery, a long black and gold brocade coat and rows and rows of pearls
and emeralds and immense hanging ear rings. She advanced to the edge of
the carpet and salaamed low. I stepped on it, made a low bow. She then
took my hand and we wandered like children down the path all carpeted
till we reached a sofa and there we sat side by side, hand in hand, with all
her women round her, and exchanged compliments.

Sunday, 26th. We went part of the way to Dachigam by motor where
H.E. had been shooting the day before. I was lucky enough to see a stag
(*barasingh*) but I was glad there were no guns. The whole place was so
beautiful it seemed sacrilege to kill. We saw for miles and miles nothing
but deep orange and bright red and old rose coloured trees and under-
growth. In the distance the mountains bright terracotta in the setting

sun and at our feet a running brook and a reservoir forming a lake. It was one of the most beautiful sights I have ever seen.

Three days of her visit were spent in bed with a bad cold and she was just able to manage a picnic on the Dal Lake and a "dull" dinner party. But this stricture is the only word of "grizzle" that creeps into her letters. She would not have enjoyed seeing a huge wounded bear coming down the hill, "bumping and grunting and rolling over and over like an enormously fat old lady in a fur coat".[2]

Back in Delhi the round of entertaining seemed "tame, after our wonderful journey to Kashmir", but she looked forward to the next tour:

> After our State visits we hope to go from Bombay to the wonderful Ellora caves and I have wanted to do that for three years, so that is something to look forward to. I am to be "dropped" at Ranjit Sinjhi's or the Jam Sahib, as we call him (it is sea side, I hear most comfortable) while H.E. chases the elusive lion in Kathiawar. Then on to Calcutta. I have to-day been arranging for 2 Balls of 500 each, one Garden Party of 2,000 and 4 dinners of 50 to 100 to start off with. The Connaughts come on 24th December. I have asked Sir Harry and Lady Lauder for Christmas Day dinner. I feel it is an inspiration on my part as most of our Staff and many of our guests are Scotch. They reign supreme in Calcutta and make all the money.

On 13th November Lady Reading writes nostalgically about the General Election at which the Conservatives returned to power, and she notes with pleasure that "our fourth Sec. of State for India[3] is fortunately a great personal friend of H.E.'s from old days at the Bar". Lord Reading was, however, to find that neither Lord Birkenhead nor the Cabinet as a whole, was prepared to go as far as he would have liked in a liberal policy in India. It is interesting to speculate on the probable progress of India towards self-government had Mr. Montagu remained in office throughout Lord Reading's Viceroyalty. It must have been immensely difficult for the man on the spot in India, the only man who could have first-hand knowledge of the immense complications involved, to sail a chosen course when buffeted by contrary winds from four different Secretaries of State in five years.

Her Ex. enjoyed meeting the Rev. Mr. Oldrieve who came to lunch:

> . . . He runs the whole Leper Settlements in India and China. My predecessor, Lady Chelmsford, had him to lunch and a General who was

rather deaf and shy sat on her other side. By way of making conversation she said to the General, "I hope you are interested in Lepers?" "Oh, yes," replied the General, "I shoot 'em by the dozen!" Tableau! Tomorrow I go to the offices we have started for 2nd National Baby Week, to hustle a bit and say a word of encouragement to the workers. I have asked for no money but sums of Rs.1,000 keep on coming in. Meanwhile I am trying to get money for a huge Eye Hospital for Delhi, am laying Foundation stone next week.

Farewell to Sir Mohammed Shafi, a friend whom they would much miss, and also a last dance for Megan, dragged home much against her will. All day long gun salutes thundered as the Princes arrived for the opening of the Chamber. When the session started the news of Edwin Montagu's death cast a deep shadow over the Readings and was mentioned with real sorrow by all the speakers. Finally, a glittering Investiture at which—

Her Ex. was the first to be decorated, and when H.E. kissed her on both cheeks the house, so to speak, rose at them. Most incorrect and entirely without precedent but delightfully spontaneous and heartfelt.[4]

On November 22nd they travelled westward to Kathiawar. This is right on the sea coast, dry sandy country north of Bombay and south-west of Rajasth'an, with the mysterious Rann of Cutch, a huge salt marsh full of creeks, to the north. To this land long ago came one of the royal tribes of Rajasth'an, the Cattis, as Colonel Tod spells them in his book. "The Catti," says Tod, "still adores [i.e. worships] the sun, scorns the peaceful arts and is much less contented with the tranquil subsistence of industry than the precarious earnings of his former predatory pursuits."[5] The chief ruling family, the Jams of Nawanagar, are descended from a Lunar line called The Induvansi, the Readings' host on this occasion being "Ranji" the famous cricketer.

Tod goes on to say, "The Catti was never happy but on horseback," and the Kathiawar horse is the most attractive and elegant indigenous Indian breed. It is the colour of treacle tart, with a black line down the back and charming ears curved inwards at the points. It is the only pure Indian horse that can compare with an Arab. The Kathiawar States were never rich in material goods, or renowned for famous architecture and scenery, but perhaps because of the nearness of the sea and the cities of the western coast, the Jam Sahib of Nawanagar and his family were friends of all the world. On the way to Rajkot, the first stop, the

Viceregal party dismounted from the train to take lunch with a small Rajah, and for tea to be garlanded by another and finally arrived, as usual, at 8.30 a.m. to find a heat wave and terrible mosquitoes. A tremendous programme included reception of all the Kathiawar Princes and princelings, and a visit to give prizes at the Rajkumar College, the oldest in India of all the schools for princely boys. Finally, a State banquet and then the Viceroy left for Junagadh and the forest of Gir where are the only lions in India. Her Ex. went on alone to Jamnagar in some trepidation for she was to have two days there carrying the whole burden of a State visit. With "Ranji" as host, she need not have worried and this visit turned out to be the happiest of her whole time in India:

Jamnagar. November 27th. I came on alone here. Found the Jam Sahib and all his nobles to meet me on the platform, a bouquet as big as my head tied with a mauve sash and all mauve bunting round the Palace. The rooms are too marvellous. This afternoon I received his sisters and nieces, Purdah ladies, and I have just come in from a drive to the sea, 7 miles away. It was good to smell the briney once more. The Jam Sahib and I are very good friends, he has the most delightful manners and is the most courteous and considerate of hosts. Many a European might take example from him!

Sunday, 30th. I have had four wonderful days, the most wonderful from my point of view that I have had in India for, in the absence of H.E., they were all *my* days. The Jam Sahib has done it all in remarkable style, cavalry escort, Royal Salute, so many gold chains to hang round my neck I felt at last like a "Buddha", so many garlands of pink roses, I looked like a Maypole.

I opened a Women's Hospital and next day visited the Orphanage. I think the Jam Sahib is rather surprised and pleased by the thorough way I do it all. Next morning he took me sightseeing. All done in a marvellous manner, he will not let me walk a step. First we went to a great temple on a Lake (deliciously cool) then to a great Jain Temple (I wrote to you before of this sect that will not take a life, not even that of a snail). Then to a factory where they make the lovely saris and embroideries, they presented me with a beauty, I bought a lot, scarves, too. In the afternoon we had a great show when I unveiled the stone to those who fell in the War, a Victory Memorial in the market place. I dined alone in my rooms as had to meet H.E. and drive in State through the City. H.E. had been lion hunting and shot a lion. He saw a lioness and her six cubs playing round the base of a tree where a buffalo had been killed. The cubs played with the buffalo like kittens, H.E. said. The Jam Sahib, I and all nobles met him on gorgeously-decorated platform, and drove through such cheering crowds, real British Hurrahs! The women looked so picturesque in bright, deep crimson with brass and copper vessels on their heads. This is supposed to bring you luck, to meet a woman thus equipped. The entire crowd, as you pass, puts both hands 2 or 3 times to ears. This means "I take on my head all the troubles of yours"! We really had a fine reception as it is the first time a Viceroy has ever been to this State.

A few hours later we drove again in State for H.E. to unveil the Memorial to Edwin Montagu designed and arranged long before his death. In bronze, by an Italian "Ricardi", a protégé of Lady Cunard's, showing him sitting in a characteristic lounging attitude with monocle in eye. The Jam Sahib read an excellent speech, then H.E. spoke beautifully, everyone very affected, his loss to India is great.

They moved on to Bombay, which is quite unlike anywhere else in India, and it is easy to miss the especial charm of the place. Alice Reading did miss it because (as so often happened) she was ill and tired. The climate is very trying to anyone not used to it, and the programme laid on for the unfortunate visitors seems far too heavy though probably a younger and stronger woman could have stood up to it. The fact that Parsee women have equal rights with men, that they are equally well educated and no purdah exists among them, makes it possible in Bombay to draw on a larger number of people for social work than anywhere else. At least this was the case in the nineteen-twenties. Then there is the sea, the real sea, right at the feet of the city. Horrible though the city is in many aspects, particularly in the "chawl" or tenement area of the mills, the glorious harbour and wide sweep of Back Bay frame Malabar Hill where even among modern blocks of flats some idea of jungle and open space persists. Here and there a bare rock protrudes, creepers grow luxuriantly and eventually you reach the end of the land and find black rocks with the sea churning and tossing around them. There are acres of palms sighing and bending, from the stinking beaches near the sewers of the city right away to Juhu and Marve, unspoilt in the Readings' day by myriads of shacks put up for the Bombay business man and his family, European and Indian, to enjoy week-ends.

However, "Heat was so terrible in Bombay," wrote Alice Reading in the train as she sped away:

... I felt too ill to write to you of our doings. When I was not out I was lying on my bed feeling like a bit of chewed string. I went to Infant Welfare

Centres, Girl Guide Rally, 2 Hospitals, on my own. Accompanied H.E. to new Cotton Factory, to the Inauguration of the Gateway of India, 2 dinner parties and a Reception to 2,300 all in three days, I was thankful to reach the train.

Yvonne describes the Gateway of India as "rather too much Wembley and not enough Moghul!" It seems odd to have copied the Moghul style at all, and the Gateway is dwarfed by the enormous harbour and distant islands. A Gateway so tremendously named should be tremendous.

On December 5th the Viceregal party travelled in some discomfort, via metre gauge, to Daulatabad in the Nizam's dominions where they motored a short distance to the pretty, cool rest house near the Cave temples of Ellora. The effect of these caves on Europeans is always interesting. Most women, for instance, find them disgusting and overwhelming. The enormous energy and intellectual effort exerted to present a religious concept in bitterly tough material demands equal energy in response and exhausts the vitality of an onlooker who has not carefully studied what the religious concept implies. These temples are carved out of the side of a rocky hill on a rise above the wide Deccan plain. The Kailasa temple is the central Brahminical monument and dates from between the third and the ninth centuries A.D. It is thought that at this time the inroads made on pure Hinduism by the branch cults of Jainism and Buddhism caused the Brahmins some anxiety and they felt a concrete expression of their difficult philosophy to be necessary in order to recapture the imagination of the people. The impression in Kailasa is of Prometheus Bound. Burning and strenuous thought controls these rock-hewn, stamping Sivas and sinuous Parvatis, these trampling elephants, lions, demons. The human brains and souls behind this work tore themselves for expression as Siva tears out the entrails of a victim. It was impossible for them to deny reality as the Jains seem to do, or to transcend it in the company of the Buddhists. God is life in all its aspects, the tender curve of Parvati's lovely body is alive and the feel of the cold stone is a shock when touched. The savage joy of Siva's dancing feet makes the ground throb and the air is stirred by his whirling arms.

Someone as sheltered and urbane as Alice Reading would be expected to recoil from these extraordinary sculptures. But she did not.

The caves were worth grilling for, cut out of the sheer solid rock, far down into the earth. Buddhas and Shivas, elephants and lions, colossal in size, perfect in preservation. The most perfect galleries with carved pilasters and columns that looked Greek to me, doorways like pierced ivory, they baffle description. The finest things I have ever seen of their kind.

She had the unconscious wisdom to leave the philosophy alone and feast her eye on line and detail and probably the sexual significance passed her by or, if she noticed it, was firmly relegated to limbo. How much better than missing the beauty because the philosophy offended!

The painted caves at Ajanta are Buddhist of a slightly earlier date than the Brahmin and Jain temples at Ellora. For centuries these monastery dwellings and places of worship lay hidden in the jungle on the side of a ravine down which a small cascade tumbles in the rainy season. The situation is incredibly wild and lonely, or was, in the Readings' day. Now it has become a favourite tourist centre much of the startling impact of coming upon these exquisite works of art at the back of beyond must be lost. They were discovered by a British officer on army exercises who broke through the jungle into the ravine about 1819. When they formed part of the Nizam's dominions the archaeological department of the state took great care of them, made wonderful tracings of those parts of the frescoes which have been destroyed by time and nature, and preserved those that remain. The government of India have carried on the work. When Lord Curzon[6] went to see them he had to travel in a *tonga*[7], but the Readings were luckier. Lord Reading was the only Viceroy other than Lord Curzon who ever went near the caves.

> We went a thirty mile drive to Ajanta. I was carried up the path to the caves by six perspiring gentlemen in torrid heat, the others climbed a mountain side covered with little green bushes and scrub and all in ridges. Then one saw what looked like a yawning black cavern. The earliest caves were plain, with carved pillars and columns, and wonderful vaulted roofs all carved out of stone. They might have come from one of our old cathedrals. The galleries carved with what looked like seraphim, but they were small Buddhas. The other caves covered in paintings, most of the colour gone but the drawing of the figures marvellously preserved.

Her Ex.'s "small Buddhas" are Apsaras, the angels of Buddhist theology. All around the standing and seated figures of the frescoes are birds and animals and plants such as one can see outside the caves.

And on the path going down the ravine the careful visitor can pick up small pieces of greenish crumbling stone which is what the monks of Ajanta used to make their green colouring. There is a poetic quality about the scenes from the life of Gautama Buddha which are the subject of these frescoes. The women are exquisite, in graceful languid poses, very simple and innocent, pastoral and pure. The monks saw as very sweet the world that they, in imitation of Gautama Buddha, renounced.

CHAPTER XVII

Round the Mulberry Bush

"And may God send you more and more
Of Garden Parties from His bounteous store."

Ode of welcome to a governor on tour.

ALICE Reading did not realise that this Christmas of 1924 was to be the last she would spend in full activity in India. Like the Simla season of the same year, the month in Calcutta teemed with events. The thirty-seventh anniversary of her wedding day passed in the train and she writes on December 10th:

> It is lovely to be here, after two years and the house [Belvedere] does look so nice; lots of grey marble and cool chintzes. The weather is like August at home, just hot sun and cool breeze. Three girls arrived to stay to-day, with Susan Binney that makes four. They have just driven off to see the sights in 2 cars with an Aide each! It's nice to be 20 at Viceregal Lodge, Calcutta. I wish I had done it earlier!!! As it is the responsibilities are so great and the work never ending, but I love it all.

The big event of Christmas Day proved to be her "Scotch Dinner" which she had been planning for weeks. Prince and Princess Arthur of Connaught[1] arrived the day before—

> ... she has grown stouter since S. Africa, has shingled her hair and wore a "flappery" dress of white piped with green, they are all staying with the Lyttons. A small dinner and big dance for them in the evening. She did not appear as was down with tummy trouble. I had him at dinner and supper. A nice fellow, not very interesting. On Christmas Day we had a splendid evening, were 40 to dinner. I sat between my friend Sir David Yule[2] and Sir Harry Lauder.[3] We had three illuminated Christmas Trees on the table and all round the room air balls with special gas. These were tied to spoons and forks and chairs and raised in mid-air. During dinner Sir Harry Lauder was writing on the Menu a bit of verse and after we had drunk the King's health brought out a little toast in honour of absent friends. Sir Victor Sassoon[4] had given all the girls monster crackers and

we had tugs of war after, with showers of gifts. Towards the end of dinner bagpipes were heard and down the long ballroom came 4 of the Cameron pipers in full dress and piped round the table. Tremendous enthusiasm amongst the many Scotch members of our party. After the crackers, Reels, Lady Lauder footing it the best of them all. I suppose she has been dancing reels all her life. Then we had Snapdragon in the Ballroom and to finish up Harry Lauder sang to us all the old favourites, "Wee deoch and dorris", "Roaming in the Gloaming", etc. It really was a success and I was pleased as Harry Lauder and the Pipers were my idea. As Sir David Yule wrote to me next day, they all said it was a "nicht of nichts".

The Begum of Bhopal has arrived to stay, her Shetland shawl over her face, and poured out all her woes to me about the succession. She wants her third son as heir (two died this year) instead of her eldest grandson.

December 28th. Yesterday evening the Lyttons gave a dinner for us and the Connaughts followed by a Reception and dance. Princess Arthur is in the latest fashion, the most abbreviated skirts, pink legs, choker pearls and the nearest approach to a shingle he will allow, he hates shaved heads! To-day, Sunday, we saw them safely off to Bikaner. They come to us five days after we return to Delhi.

December 31st. To-night a thousand guests to a Fancy Dress Ball. I start at 8 to-morrow to drive in State to the Proclamation Parade. Then home to rest and we lunch with the Stewards of the Royal Calcutta Turf Club before the Races. I have cried Halt to accompanying H.E. to the Horse Show and the Warship *Chatham* this morning. I finished up yesterday with a Purdah Party at the Maharani of Cooch Behar,[5] a most attractive lady with lovely children acting in Indian tableaux. Then I went to bed but H.E. and entire party went to the Scottish Ball and most of them danced half the night. I shall be glad when I get them all safely back to Delhi. A London season is not in it for dissipation.

January 7th, 1925. Nearly off again, we leave to-morrow night after the most strenuous month even I have ever experienced in India. I feel in a state of collapse and only the interest and amusement has carried me through. Much as I like Delhi I can understand why Calcutta is still so sore that the Viceroy was removed from here. It makes all the difference in the world to Calcutta if we are here.

In addition to the functions Lady Reading carried out her usual visits to hospitals, health centres and schools. A Tibetan General and his wife and niece came to lunch—

. . . He sat next to me dressed in orange with a funny little hat on an elastic. Next to him an Interpreter as he speaks no English but we got on splendidly and he gave me a warm invitation to Tibet, while promising to come and see us again at Delhi. His wife was fascinating, with her mother's and grandmother's *hairs* in a mane round her head finishing with turqoises, chunks of turqoises from ear to shoulder, plaques of it round her neck, a lovely orange bodice with peacock blue striped Tibetan skirt. A merry twinkle in her eye. A very attractive niece in a fur cap, with bobbed hair, who spoke English.

Everyone very eulogistic about my "Baby Week" which is flourishing and continually fed by cheques of 5 and 10,000 rupees.

Sir Victor Sassoon had given a vast sum of money (she never actually mentions how much) for her to administer and as soon as the fact was known appeals flowed in from all and sundry.

The strain of Calcutta took its toll and laid Her Ex. low with 'flu the moment she got back to Delhi, and she was only just able to get up to receive the Connaughts—

... I know few things more horrible than the after-effects of 'flu. Every time anyone comes in to ask me a question (and this happens every few minutes) I want to throw the ink at them. To-morrow the Connaughts arrive with Aide, Valet and maid, also Mrs. Jack Tennant and daughter, Sir Warden Chilcote,[6] Sir Robert Horne,[7] the Mosleys[8] (she was a Curzon), the Dalkeiths[9] and about a dozen other people at intervals of a day or two including the Goschens[10] from Madras (the new Governor) and several Americans. Our garden is bristling with tents.

As I write Miss Fitzroy comes in with letters, Susan with inquiries, Sister with medicine, Captain Burton[11] with invitation lists, all through three doors at once, it's like a French farce but less funny, as I feel today! I must stop and go back to bed so as to look my beautifulest to-morrow.

The Connaughts' visit was a success. Alice Reading seems to have had the gift of making people feel "at home" even in the midst of endless functions. The Pavilion built for the Prince of Wales helped to give V.I.P.s some privacy and seclusion. Her comments on some of the visitors are interesting, particularly in the light of later events in which some of them were to be involved:

I think Sir Robert Horne is one of our nicest visitors. He has the most marvellous spirits and is a wonderful raconteur, the life and soul of any party. Lady Cynthia Mosley is charming, he is clever but a strange, weird creature, I don't like his friends. He has had interviews with Gandhi, I don't mind him, but with C. R. Das and others whom I cordially dislike.

Lady Cynthia is really very handsome, very attractive. He is less handsome and less attractive!! One excitement has been an Italian Opera Company. They did not lure me there till last night when *La Tosca* was given. I was much amused at the following conversation between Aides: "Does anyone know anything of this play to-night, *La Tosca*?" *Another*: "Of course, everyone knows Tosca's Goodbye!" *3rd Aide* (quick as lightning): "Yes, they sing Land of Hope and Glory in the first Act." We took the Begum of Bhopal who had never been to an opera before and was much thrilled by the love-making. The Begum and I interview each other daily, she does not take meals with us but her cooks concoct dishes in the back verandah. The only woman ruler in India and I think it is dust and ashes for her. She is a born autocrat and no-one in her State dares oppose her. These Rulers have a wonderful position and enormous power, which makes it all the more tragic if they do not use it well. She complained yesterday that though she was enjoying herself she had not enough to do. She sallies forth before 8 a.m. to the mosque, and prays at intervals during the day, being a very devout Mahommedan. The Legislative Assembly is sitting, but they don't seem to get much forrarder. Sastri has gone, his health was so bad, it is a pity for his was a rare intellect. I am terribly busy with National Baby Week, I've set my heart on making it a great success this year, money is coming in daily, unsolicited.

I was sorry when the Connaughts left. They really are a charming couple and appreciative, and after she got over her terrible shyness she enjoyed every minute of her stay. It is a pity people like that are born in the purple, for as plain Mr. and Mrs. they would be happier. They hate show and ceremonies and being fussed over. I think they enjoyed this visit as we left them to do what they liked all day and only had State functions at night. She told me she would love to buy my little Pavilion and live there always in the midst of the beautiful garden with sunshine and blue skies, allowed to do what she loves, shooting, walking, playing tennis and acting. She is a splendid shot with a rifle.

Sunday, February 9th. I am writing this Sunday morning in bed at Gujner (Bikaner), my bed a few feet only from the window and under the window the lake where now, 7.45, already the guns are pop-popping as they are shooting sandgrouse. I believe it was a "record bag" yesterday, 3,200 in one morning. I hate to see the slaughter so instead of going with the guns I have been exploring the wonderful garden, right in the midst of the desert. I should like to stop a week but we are off again tonight after dinner.

February 11th. Back in Delhi, the opening of National Baby Week gone off all right. We had a big show and what pleased me most, Swarajists on the platform. One thing we sink all differences over is the Infant Welfare question. I have a tremendous week, three times to the Show and then close it on Saturday, and on Sunday 12 miles out to New Delhi to see the Coolies' wives and children.

Her Ex.'s next letter, in wavering hand-writing, is dated February 28th and tells of days in bed with a feverish chill caught at a Church Bazaar, followed up by a huge Ball and a Torchlight Tattoo. She then took to her bed leaving a —

. . . houseful of visitors to their fate. Sir Edwin Lutyens, who is staying here, cheers me up by the maddest drawings sent through Sister. The latest is, "Baby's Weak in the Jungle" with all the Aides as wild animals and all that is seen of H.E. and me is one natty pair of shoes, and one pair of rough shooting boots hanging from a branch. He is as mad as a hatter, but very amusing. He told us when first New Delhi was contemplated they had a meeting of an Indian and European Committee and the question came up, what the new City was to be called? It was in June with a temp. of 117 in the shade. No-one could make up their minds. At last a voice came from Sir Edwin, "Why not Uzipore? (ooze-a-pore)" The meeting broke up in confusion saying he was hopeless and so he is like many geniuses.

March 3rd. Still in bed after 10 days, strange to relate everything seems to go on without me. Our house is still full of such nice guests that it makes it doubly irritating. If all goes well we hope to sail on April 11th and reach Marseilles about the 26th. I cannot grasp it yet, I have thought of it so long and so often and now it has come so suddenly. I have a terrible lot to do before we start and must get strong, else you will not believe all the stories you have been told about my youth, and prowess, my work, dancing, etc.

Lord Reading was the first Viceroy ever to take leave during his term of office and an Act of Parliament had to be passed to make it possible for him to do so. He wanted to discuss the progress of the constitutional reforms with the Cabinet and he also felt that both he and his wife badly needed a rest. There had been two occasions before when a period of leave was mooted and then discarded, and she then had showed great disappointment. Now the full tide of her position had her in its grip and she did not want to break loose. She may have felt that if she once stopped she might not be able to start again. On March 11th the Viceroy and a party went, as usual, to Agra but Her Ex. was not well enough to go:

I spent the week end at home with Sister, Miss F., my Aide. It was a terrible disappointment missing Agra, as this is a yearly pilgrimage and one I look forward to so much, but I hope for better luck next year. I used my time looking through hundreds of applications from people hoping to get a crumb of Sir Victor Sassoon's bounty. It is a terrible task to tackle as appeals pour in from all parts of India, from a woman who wants a new sari or a set of false teeth to Institutions who coolly ask for £10,000 to enlarge their premises. Sir Victor told me he was having a lovely time, for applications streamed in to him and he has had a slip printed on which he says, "Kindly refer to Her Ex. in whose hands I have placed the money unreservedly."

We have the "Plymouth Brethren", as I call them, here at present. Young Lord Plymouth[12] with a very attractive wife, a mother, mother-in-law, married sister and four maids. He has been travelling round India with a regular harem. His mother-in-law, old Lady Wemyss, has a foible for reading aloud and insists on reading Indian history to them by the hour together, even in a railway carriage! Still, Lord Plymouth seems a cheerful soul.

I have had quite a field day to-day, Burma's Governor sent me a charming bronze statuette of a woman and child out of gratitude for Baby Week and in the afternoon an Indian lady, wife of one of H.E.'s Councillors of State, arrived in Purdah and tears with yards of embroidery worked by her own fair hands, and every time I ring for my Bearer he says, "Me go to England too, yes?" Our visitors still continue and I honestly believe that on the eve of our departure we shall have a fresh contingent and it is getting very difficult as the heat in the tents is so great we have to put a lot of Secretaries in the house. I am better and at work, my first outing to Hardinge College to give the girls their prizes. Everyone has been so good to me. I have reached £140,000 now and have money for all my Indian enterprises.

March 24th. A gloom cast over everyone by Curzon's death. Sunday we had a Memorial Service, none too impressive as our clergyman was away ill and the choir all laid up with various ailments, and the man who officiated had very little time to prepare and was painfully nervous.

Lord Lytton came to talk over things with H.E. It seems so strange to think he will be at Simla and we so far away from all our activities. I shall miss my Hospital. The head Dr. came here on Monday for last instructions. We are adding a little annexe with rooms for 2 European Staff Nurses and five Indians. Four of my eight nurses have already passed their exams, when the other four pass I have promised them a gramophone, they already have a piano and their own native instruments.

General Birdwood's[13] appointment as Lord Rawlinson's successor as

Commander-in-Chief in India has been announced and greatly approved. Unfortunately Lord Rawlinson is ill and we are all rather worried about him.

Lord Rawlinson and Lord Reading worked together harmoniously and "Rawly" was very popular with all ranks, colours and races. He amused Lady Reading, teased her when she became too starched and touched her heart by riding out to Mashobra to paint a picture of "The Retreat" as a birthday present for her. He was a soldier of many gifts and played polo and hunted the boar along with his staff, who all greatly loved him. In her last letter before going down to Bombay, Alice Reading tells of his death. He died in Delhi after a major operation:

> The whole week has been overshadowed by the terrible fear that the C.-in-C. would not recover. Alas! The worst has happened. He died this morning. We have lived for the last four years in such close touch with him and his household, we all feel we have lost one of our best friends, and for H.E. the loss is greatest, they worked so much together.
>
> It is very miserable in Delhi. I am glad we are leaving and this is my last mail. I shall not know what to do with myself on Thursdays without 12 to 15 letters to write or finish. We leave here on the 9th and directly we arrive at Bombay board the *Razmak*. I hear of all sorts of luxuries, a cow for me, cabins specially decorated by Elsie Mackay, Lord Inchcape's daughter. We do not stop at Aden as we burn oil so have not to coal. We leave England to return here on July 22nd or 23rd and (D.V.) arrive Bombay, a molten mass and very seasick, on August 7th. The only thing I am dreading is the return journey but I made a condition of coming home that nothing should be put in my way for my return here with H.E. as I would *never* allow him to come alone.
>
> I shall miss my flowers, my room is a mass of pink roses and lilies. H.E. leaves to-morrow night for a few days' tiger shoot at Rewa. He has had to disappoint the Maharajah twice so I am glad he is going. We can only work here before 11 a.m. or after 7 at night, the heat is so great, but it is still bearable with fans and an enormous lump of ice. Also "*khuskhus*" (aromatic matting) which is wetted and the air drawn through. These we use as blinds in the railway carriages, else heat would be unbearable on the glass. Well, well, I shall have a good many cool days in England.

So they set sail for home and on the deck of the *Razmak* a small tent had been prepared for their shelter containing two red and gold chairs of State for use at the farewell ceremonies in port. So exhausted were both the Readings that after the shore of India vanished over the horizon, they fell asleep where they sat and a friend, coming to see if all was well, found them there, hand-in-hand.

CHAPTER XVIII

Hail and Farewell

"Kalam in ja rasid o sar bi-shikast — The Pen arrived thus far and broke
its point."

Indian Proverb

THE final letters preserved in Alice Reading's own hand are
from Simla after her return in August, 1925:

11 August. I am only up for a few hours as feel the height very
much and am also recovering from the effects of that ghastly nightmare of a
journey. When I had completed it I felt inclined to echo many people and
say to myself, "You brave woman!" but I had to be honest and acknowledge
if I had known what it was going to be like I could never have gone through
with it. I am trying to forget now the horrible week from Aden to Bombay,
particularly when I slept (?) with a bath towel at my feet as every few
minutes I had to get dry; and then the journey from Bombay to Kalka by
train!!!!! I counted 50 animals on my bed. I killed up to 4 in the morning,
some as big as black beetles. The stirring welcome and reception we got at
Simla compensated for much and now I am delighted to be back again
and shall be more pleased when I can get into harness once more. In spite
of private arrival a crowd of people came to welcome us and what pleased
me more was that all the poor people came out of their bazaars and covered
the hills and roads right up to Viceregal Lodge.

There seems to be some emotional feeling over C. R. Das's death, but
when I think of 4 years ago and our arrival here then we have every reason
to be pleased at the turn of events under H.E.'s wise guidance.

The death of Mr. C. R. Das weakened the extremist section of the
Swaraj party, which now moved nearer to co-operation with the
Government. Lord Birkenhead's speech (on July 7th of that year) had,
in fact, been more conciliatory than anyone in India anticipated. He
invited Indians to "produce a Constitution which carried behind it a
fair measure of general agreement among the great peoples of India."
Lord Reading always wanted to proceed more quickly than the Cabinet
at home would allow and it is tempting to speculate on whether future

164

misunderstanding could have been avoided if he had been given a free hand.

Lady Reading naturally hurried to her hospital as soon as she was well enough to do so:

... The first break in the clouds I went to my Hospital to see the new Nurses' quarters and visit all the patients. Great excitement! One Indian lady in the paying ward had changed her costume already 6 times that morning in my honour. They were all pleased to see me and it all looked so beautiful and so well kept? My Dr. Hamilton is a veritable genius of a doctor! She lunched here to-day but was called away as a new Baby was arriving. How she manages the work of 69 patients is a mystery to me!

The usual Balls, dinners and lunches succeeded each other, but she missed "many old friends, some dead, some on leave. India is a bad place for partings."

The Viceroy delivered an exceptionally warm-hearted and conciliatory speech when opening the Legislative Assembly, of which Her Ex. writes:

The C.-in-C. [General Sir William Birdwood] sent me a letter as soon as it was over saying, "I feel I must tell you how really grand the Viceroy's speech was, indeed a magnificent effort in the way of great delivery and expression, it will go down in history as of the greatest delivered by any Viceroy." I think he was right.

I have not been very well this last fortnight which makes life rather difficult as entertaining and functions must go on just the same. Sir Frederick Whyte,[1] the retiring President of Assembly, is being greatly fêted and we give a dinner on Sept. 4th of over 80 Members in his honour. They have just elected a Swarajist Member in his stead (Mr. V. J. Patel[2]). He renounced his extreme views in his opening speech and was kind enough to say that if the Viceroy sent for him 10 times a day he would obey the summons. When we were in Bombay (he comes from there) he refused to join in an address of welcome to H.E. though he was careful to say it was not because of the man, only the politics. This all makes the sitting of the Assembly interesting, and a great change, to my mind, has come over them and I cannot help thinking that if we were to be longer here there would be further co-operation.

Thus, publicly, the Readings began to reap the results of their joint labours. For she had done her part as surely as he. The effort, even though she enjoyed it, took greater toll of her health than even she recognised. If she became more imperious and aloof, more irritable and exacting, her waning strength excuses her. Shutting herself away from all but those functions that were necessary, she only gave of her best to those who meant most to her. People now grown old who were on her Staff, speak of her as distant and alarming, but they all respected her, and also loved her when she gave them a chance to get near enough to know her gentler side. She never encouraged an informal or romping atmosphere. As well as deafness, her age must be considered and a secluded and formal upbringing. Writing on September 9th she gives a glimpse of a benign mood:

> A very good dance, though small, on Friday for two engaged couples. The two young men sat on either side of me and Simla gossip said they had nervous prostration at the prospect and my horrid Aides reported their teeth were chattering before we came down to dinner. I don't know if it was a good dinner and champagne, or if I did not prove as fierce as I was painted, but by the second course they were chattering away and confiding in me all their hopes and fears for the future.

One wet Sunday, when the monsoon blocked the road to Mashobra, she took her husband to inspect the hospital with her:

> H.E. came with me on my weekly visit. He was delighted with it all and said so many nice things about its organisation and the way it is run that my cup of happiness was brimming over. One of the Indian members of the Municipality spoke to him and said all India was talking of it, it was the first time in his 50 years that the men had brought in their wives to hospital, some on their backs from the Hills. I *was* pleased as I have had such an uphill fight and even now when I am determined to build extra rooms for Nurses I can get no water laid on, everything has to come from the main building. Still, I have stirred them up a bit as before I go I am going to build a new Out-Patients' Dept. as the sick have to wait about in the rain, there is no accommodation and I appealed to the Municipality to get my plans signed and sealed in 6 days. They did it, building started on the 7th day!

Her sincerity and freedom from prejudice produced sincerity in return; what the municipal councillor said about husbands bringing their wives into hospital was quite true; it was an unusual development in those days among the poorer classes, and especially the shy people of the Hills. Quite well-meaning Europeans, doctors among them, did not hesitate to say of inadequate hospital conditions, "It does not matter, this is what they are used to at home." But Alice Reading would not have enjoyed waiting in the rain for attention, her grandchildren appreciated toys when convalescent, her friends expected good beds and clean rooms. Therefore all these things must be given to those for whom she felt responsibility and affection, the women and children of India. She looked ahead to Baby Week 1926 and regretted the departure of Lady Whyte, "she has been a great help to me, has a level Scotch head, very intelligent. Her absence will make more work for me at Delhi Baby Week in January; we always ran it together."

The Begum of Bhopal dashed up to Simla to talk over her troubles and to draw strength from her "esteemed friend" before embarking for England to take up the matter of the succession in her state with the King Emperor himself. The farewell dinner to the Whytes proved to be very exhausting:

... 88 to dinner and it was a task afterwards. About a dozen women first to talk to, then till 11.30 one man after another, Indians and Europeans, switched on for 4 or 5 minutes among them Patel the Swarajist, President of the Legislative Assembly, in full *"Khaddar"*. A merry twinkle in his eye! The next day I opened the Catholic Fête which always excites fury on the part of the other Churches as they get most of their money by playing games of chance perilously like Roulette and Boule, etc.

The Military Secretary left yesterday to meet the King and Queen of the Belgians [King Albert and Queen Elisabeth] at Bombay. They go to Poona, Calcutta, and Darjeeling, then to Delhi and Agra as our guests, we have opened V. Lodge for them. Then up here on October 3rd. They have asked for a private visit, so we will only give one big Ball. We stay here till October 20th this year and then go to Baluchistan. I don't think there is much to see, the whole town of Quetta cannot produce a closed car but I love seeing new places and people. It is the travelling that is so wearying! But how I shall long for my beautiful train in years to come!

We have had Maharajahs of Bikaner, Alwar, Dholpur and their Staffs staying here, the house is full of strange men, the retainers in velvet and gold, curry is served at every odd moment. We had promised to attend a Carnival dance for the Church [of England] and set forth for an hour accompanied by 2 or 3 Maharajahs. Alwar elected to stay at home as he was in mourning for his "Grandma", all in black with his moustache gone and head shaved, but on his last night he relented as to the black and appeared gorgeous in dark blue and gold with a diamond necklace, ear-rings and bracelet.

She ends abruptly, in rather a quavering hand, as she had just received news of the death of a very dear friend in England. The last letter in the collection is dated September 20th–23rd:

> I am just in the throes of arranging a huge, farewell Purdah Party, always an anxious business as the Indian ladies either do not answer at all, or at the very last minute. This finishes the entertaining excepting a dinner to outgoing members of Council, a dinner, last night to the Belgian King and Queen and a Ball of 700 the night before they leave. Then I must think of packing up — — never to return.

Just before the arrival of King Albert and Queen Elisabeth, Alice Reading learnt from her doctor that she would have to undergo a major operation as soon as possible. Characteristically, she said nothing to her husband till they were on their way back from Summer Hill station after seeing the Belgian party depart. All through that Ball for 700, all through the days of attendance on Royalty, she must have greatly endured.

So she never went to Baluchistan, but to Calcutta instead, where the operation was performed and for a long time she lay dangerously ill. She appeared for the State drive on the racecourse on Viceroy's Cup day and received an ovation not only from the expensive stands, but all along the course past the cheap enclosures where the real people of India took their pleasure. An event of this nature she would regard as her husband's triumph rather than her own.

There is no more evidence in her own hand after that final sentence written in Simla in September, 1925. After a lifetime of constant ill-health in the background of her husband's glittering career, she stepped out into a blaze of power and energy when she came to India. This was a task which she could fully share with him, in which her part was essential. This sharing, this demand, gave her strength to surmount her fragile health. It is interesting to find that Sir Francis Oppenheimer, at the beginning of her married life, and Lady Lee of Fareham who met her near the end of it, came to the same conclusion. That without her unfailing faith and unwavering determination her husband might never have used his great gifts to the full and reached the summit. It would seem that she fused her love for and pride in her husband with a love for, and deep interest in, the people of India; the poor people, the rich people, the colours, smells, sounds, flowers, hills, trees, animals even insects of India. Alice Reading knew nothing about them all when she arrived, and had not time to learn more than a little before she left. But she made her mark because she felt at home; she gave her heart and may have left some of it behind as many of us have done before and since. The gift of the heart is one that India never refuses or denies.

Notes

CHAPTER I

Pages 21-26

1. *Purdah.* The word means "curtain". Term used to denote seclusion of women in an Indian family.
2. Edwin Montagu (1879–1924). Second son of 1st Lord Swaythling. Parliamentary Secretary to H. H. Asquith when Prime Minister, 1908–10. Parliamentary Under-Secretary of State for India, 1910–14. Financial Secretary to the Treasury, 1914–16. Minister of Munitions, 1916. Secretary of State for India, 1917–22.
3. Frederick John Napier, Baron Chelmsford, G.C.S.I., G.C.M.G. Viceroy of India, 1916–21. Created Viscount, 1921.
4. Comte Ségur.
5. *Stranger Within* by Sir Francis Oppenheimer (Faber, 1960), p. 99.
6. *Idem.*
7. Letter from Sir Harcourt Butler, April 14th, 1921. Spencer Harcourt Butler, G.C.S.I., G.C.I.E., F.R.G.S., F.R.S.A., F.R.A.S., F.Z.S., (1869–1938). Lt. Governor of Burma, 1915–17. Lt. Governor, later Governor of United Provinces of Agra and Oudh, 1918–1925. Governor of Burma, 1925–27. Chairman, Indian States Committee, 1928.

CHAPTER II

Pages 27-35

1. Gerald Rufus, 2nd Marquess of Reading (1889–1960). Under-Secretary for Foreign Affairs, 1951–53. Minister of State, 1953–57. Mentioned in Despatches, Croix de Guerre in World War I. Privy Councillor, 1953. K.C.M.G., 1957, G.C.M.G., 1958. He married Eva Violet Mond, C.B.E., J.P., eldest daughter of the 1st Lord Melchett.
2. Yvonne FitzRoy. Only daughter of Sir Almeric FitzRoy, Clerk to the Privy Council. Private Secretary to Lady Reading, 1921–25. Author of *Courts and Camps in India* (Methuen, 1926).
3. Dorothy, C.I., D.C.V.O., daughter of the 4th Earl of Onslow. Wife of Edward Wood, Baron Irwin, later 1st Earl of Halifax and the Viceroy of India, 1926–31.
4. Marie Adelaide, G.B.E., C.I., Kaiser-i-Hind Medal, daughter of the 1st Earl Brassey, wife of Freeman Freeman-Thomas, 1st Marquess of Willingdon, Viceroy of India, 1931–36.
5. Doreen, C.I., daughter of Sir Frederick Milner, wife of Victor Alexander John, 2nd Marquess of Linlithgow, Viceroy of India, 1936–41.
6. *The Garden of Allah:* a play by Robert Hichens popular in London in the early nineteen-twenties. In one scene a realistic sandstorm scattered dust over the stalls.
7. *Simla Past and Present* by Edward J. Buck (Times of India Press, Bombay, 1925).
8. *Idem.*

9. Lord William Cavendish Bentinck. Second son of the 3rd Duke of Portland. Governor of Madras, 1806. Governor-General of India, 1828–35. Abolished *suttee* (the immolation of Hindu widows), also flogging in the Indian Army. Founded Calcutta Medical College, 1835.
10. John Laird Mair Lawrence (1811–79). Born in Dublin. Joined the Bengal Army and was posted to Northern India. Became a civil administrator and the founder of the Punjaub. Except for Warren Hastings, the only member of the Civil Service to become Governor-General (1864–69). Raised to the Peerage.
11. Mohandas Karamchand Gandhi (1869–1948). Called to the Bar, 1889. Practised till 1908 when he gave up to become champion of the rights of Indians in South Africa. Returned to India in 1915. Started non-co-operation movement in India, 1920. Inaugurated Civil Disobedience Campaign, 1930. Assassinated at a prayer meeting, 1948. Styled *Mahatma* ('Great Soul'). Exponent of *satyagraha* (passive resistance).
12. Sister Meikle, a trained nurse, came to India as part of Lady Reading's personal staff, by order of her doctor.

CHAPTER III

Pages 36–42

1. Indian National Congress: met for the first time in Bombay, 1885. From then on worked for inclusion of Indians in government and finally for independence. Now the major political party in India.
2. Maulana Mahommed Ali (1878–1931). Educated Aligarh College and University. Matriculated Lincoln College, Oxford. Became a journalist; published and edited *The Comrade*, a Muslim weekly written in English. Interned 1914–18 because of sympathy with Turkey and again because of support of Afghanistan in Afghan War of 1919–20. Released on introduction of Montagu-Chelmsford Reforms. Founded Khilafat movement in support of Turkish rights after the war and religious leadership of the Khilafa, but when the Turks deprived the latter of his spiritual power, the Ali brothers joined the more moderate section of Muslim opinion.
   Maulana Shaukat Ali, brother of the above, was born in 1873; he followed much the same career.
3. This Treaty was concerned with Turkey's part against the Allies in World War I. The terms were very hard which exacerbated Muslim opinion everywhere.
4. The Moplahs, or Mapillahs, were a fanatical sect of Arab origin living in Malabar, South India. They were stirred up by the Khilafat agitation and fell upon the local police and then their Hindu neighbours. The revolt and subsequent massacres were suppressed with great severity.
5. Mian Mahommed Shafi, K.C.S.I., C.I.E., (1869–1932). Founder of the Punjaub Muslim Association which merged into the All India Muslim League. Called to the Bar, Middle Temple, 1892. President of the All India Muslim League in 1913 and 1927. Education Member, Viceroy's Executive Council, 1919–22. Knighted, 1922. Legal Member of the Executive Council, 1923–24.
6. They originally carried a palanquin called a *jampan*.
7. Afternoon tea-party for ladies only.
8. Mary Mond, second daughter of Alfred Mond, 1st Lord Melchett (1868–1930). Sister of Viscountess Erleigh, Lady Reading's daughter-in-law.
9. Her Highness Nawab Sultan Jehan Begum, G.C.I.E., G.B.E. Succeeded her mother in 1901. Direct descendant of Dost Mahommed, an Afghan soldier of fortune who came to India in 1697 and died in 1726 leaving a well-established state in Central India

behind him. By the time of the Sepoy Mutiny (1857), the ladies of the family had the government of the state in their hands and decided to support the British. Lord Canning confirmed their rulership and three generations of Begums came to an end with the subject of this note who abdicated in favour of her third son, Mahommed Hamidullah, in 1926 and died in 1930.

10. Sir John Maffey, K.C.V.O., C.S.I., C.I.E., Chief Commissioner, North-West Frontier Province, 1921–24.

CHAPTER IV

Pages 43–49

1. His Highness Raj Rajeshwar Shri Sawai Maharaj Lt. Colonel Sir Jai Singhji Veerendra Shiromani Dev Deo, G.C.S.I., G.C.I.E., (1882–1937), Maharajah of Alwar. Honorary Colonel in the British Army. Succeeded 1892. Area of State, 3,185 square miles; population, 703,382.

2. Indian proverb implying counterfeit.

3. William Eugene Johnson (1862–1945). Known as "Pussyfoot" because of his cat-like policies in pursuing law-breakers in (American) Indian territory. A professional journalist who devoted himself to furthering the cause of temperance. Became special agent to the Department of the Interior (U.S. Government) to enforce prohibition laws in Indian territory and Oklahoma, 1906–1907. Directed the London office of the World League against Alcoholism, 1916–18. Life member, Prohibition League of India. Lost an eye at a prohibition meeting in Essex Hall, London, because of a missile thrown by one of the mob. Round the world three times in the interest of temperance.

CHAPTER V

Pages 50–56

1. John Nicholson (1822–58). Born in Dublin. Joined Bengal Infantry at the age of sixteen and was posted to the Punjaub. After a distinguished career as soldier and civil administrator, he led Sikh troops to the relief of Delhi in 1858 and was killed while personally leading the assault on the Kashmir Gate.

2. James Skinner (1778–1841). Son of a Scottish Ensign and a Rajput lady. Served under General de Boigne, Commander of Scindia's army in the Mahratta Wars. After the collapse of Mahratta power he was employed by the British and founded a corps of irregular horse ("The Yellow Boys"), now the Ist Lancers (Skinner's Horse), Indian Army. Helped to consolidate British power in India. Retired to a large estate at Hansi, near Delhi. Built St. James's Church just inside the Kashmir Gate, Delhi. Known far and wide as "Sikander Sahib".

3. Kurram Shihab-ud-din Mahommed (1592–1666) succeeded as Shah Jehan, fifth Emperor of the Timurid (Moghul) dynasty. Reigned from 1627–88 when he was deposed and imprisoned by his son, Aurangzebe. Built the Taj Mahal at Agra and the Red Fort at Delhi.

4. The custom of Indian Rulers to show themselves to the people at regular intervals.

5. Mahommed Humayon (1507–56), second Emperor of the Timurid (Moghul) dynasty. Succeeded his father, Zahir-ud-din Babur in 1530. Had to fight his brothers for the throne. Died as the result of a fall on the steep steps of his library in the Purana Khila (Old Fort) at Delhi.

6. His Highness Sir Pratab Singh, Maharajah of Jammu and Kashmir, G.C.S.I., G.C.I.E., G.B.E., (1850–1925). Ruled over 3,300,000 square miles.

7. His Highness Sir Ganga Singh, Maharajah of Bikaner, G.C.S.I., G.C.I.E., G.C.V.O., G.B.E. (1880–1943). Succeeded at the age of seven years. Served in China commanding Bikaner Camel Corps, 1900–1901. Knighted in 1901. Mentioned in despatches twice in World War I. Represented India at the Imperial War Cabinet, 1917, and the Paris Peace Conference, 1919. Led the Indian delegation to the League of Nations, 1930. First Chancellor of the Chamber of Princes, 1921–26. General in the British Army, 1927. Chancellor of Benares Hindu University, 1929–43.

8. His Highness Maharajah Scindia of Gwalior, Madhava Rao II, G.C.V.O., G.C.S.I. (1886–1925). Organised and financed a hospital ship in World War I. Aide-de-camp to the King.

9. His Highness Jagatji Singh, Maharajah of Kapurthala, G.C.S.I., G.C.I.E., G.B.E. (1872–1949). Succeeded at the age of five. Ruled over 878,880 people. Area of state, 652 square miles. Promoted from Rajah to Maharajah in 1911.

10. His Highness Maharajah Jam Sahib Kumar Shri Ranjitsinhji of Nawanagar, K.C.S.I., G.B.E. Born 1872. Honorary Lt. Colonel in the British Army. Succeeded his cousin, 1906. Educated Trinity College, Cambridge. Played first for Sussex County Cricket Club, 1895; head of averages for that year. Champion batsman for all England, 1896 and 1900, scoring 2,780 runs with an average of 59–81. Served in World War I. Lent his house at Staines for a military hospital.

11. Arthur William Patrick Albert, 1st Duke of Connaught, K.G. (1850–1942), third son of Queen Victoria. Governor-General of Canada, 1911–16.

12. Country house for Warren Hastings, Governor-General from 1774 to 1785. Remained the country residence of Governors-General until the move to Delhi, after which it was reserved for the use of the Viceroy on his visits to Calcutta.

13. Gilbert Elliot, 4th Earl of Minto, P.C., G.C.S.I., G.C.M.G., G.C.I.E., (1898–1914). Viceroy of India, 1905–10.

14. His Highness Sir Shuja-ul-Mulk, 16th Mehtar of Chitral, a hill state on the borders of Kashmir.

15. Charles Kenneth Howard Bury, D.S.O. (1883–1963). Leader of the first Everest expedition, 1921. Fellow of the Royal Geographical Society. Member of Parliament, 1920–31.

16. A large military station about forty-five miles north-east of Delhi. The Sepoy Mutiny broke out here in Indian Cavalry Lines when all British troops were in church.

17. An appeal launched by Lady Chelmsford in 1919 for funds for maternity and child welfare work.

18. An association founded in 1906 by Mary, Countess of Minto, to provide nursing care for European families. Wound up in 1947.

19. The Lady Hardinge Medical College for Women was originally called the Lady Hardinge Hospital. She was the wife of Charles, Baron Hardinge of Penshurst, Viceroy of India, 1910–16, and raised 30 lakhs to celebrate the visit of Queen Mary to India in 1911. After Lady Hardinge's death in 1915, the name was changed as a memorial to her and the hospital developed into a medical school for women, the first of its kind. It taught up to the standard of M.B., B.S., and a training school for nurses was inaugurated at the same time.

20. His Highness Sayaji Rao III. Gaekwar of Baroda, G.C.S.I., G.C.I.E. (1863–1939). Adopted after the deposition of Malhar Rao, 1875.

CHAPTER VI

Pages 57–62

1. *The Continent of Circe* by Niraud Chaudhuri (Chatto and Windus, 1965), p. 35.
2. His Highness Sir Prabhu Narayan Singh, Maharajah of Benares (1885–1931). Succeeded 1889.
3. Richard Wellesley, Baron Wellesley in the Peerage of Great Britain, Earl of Mornington in the Peerage of Ireland. Later Marquess Wellesley. Governor-General, 1798–1805. Elder brother of Arthur Wellesley, Duke of Wellington.
4. Her grandchildren, Michael, Joan and Elizabeth Rufus Isaacs – now the 3rd Marquess of Reading, the Lady Joan Zuckerman and the Lady Elizabeth Hornsby.
5. Dame Margaret Helen Anderson, D.B.E. (1922), daughter of William McEwan, M.P. for Central Edinburgh. Widow of the Hon. R. Greville (died 1908), eldest son of 2nd Baron Greville. She died September, 1942.
6. Sir Henry Dodds, British Ambassador to Afghanistan.
7. A play by J. M. Barrie which had some success in London at the end of the War. The Cinderella story was played as a charade within a play and in the ball scene the characters pranced round the room like horses with plumes on their heads, waving to the King and Queen.
8. Laurence Dundas, Earl of Ronaldshay, later 2nd Marquess of Zetland, G.C.S.I., G.C.I.E., (1876–1961). Governor of Bengal, 1917–22. Secretary of State for India, 1935–40.

CHAPTER VII

Pages 63–72

1. Nur-ud-din Mahommed Jehangir (1569–1627), fourth Emperor of the Timurid (Moghul) dynasty. Son of Akbar the Great by a Rajput lady. Succeeded in 1605.
2. *Kubla Khan* by Samuel Taylor Coleridge.
3. Throne.
4. His Highness Sir Sawai Madho Singh Bahadur, G.C.S.I., G.C.I.E., G.C.V.O., G.B.E. (1861–1922). Succeeded 1880. Ruler over 15,000 square miles and 2,700,000 people.
5. Heir. Lt.-General H. H. Saramad-i-Rajahal Hindustan Raj Rajendra Shri Maharajad-hiraj Sir Sawai Man Singh Bahadur, Maharajah of Jaipur, G.C.S.I., G.C.I.E. Thirty-ninth ruler of Indian State of Jaipur and head of the Kachhawa clan of Rajputs. Born 1911. Adopted son of Lt.-General Maharaja Sir Sawai Madho Singh Bahadur whom he succeeded in 1922. Full ruling powers, 1931. Honorary Lt.-General Indian Army. Commissioned in H.M.'s Life Guards, 1939. Attended Staff College, Quetta, 1943. Rajpramukh of Rajasth'an, 1949–56. Elected Member of Raja Sabha, 1962. Ambassador in Spain, 1965–68. International polo player (took team to England, 1933; set up record by winning all open tournaments; led Indian Polo Team which won Gold Cup at Deauville, 1957).
6. The ancient capital and chief fortress of the state, abandoned when Sawai Jai Singh built his new city.

CHAPTER VIII

Pages 73–81

1. Cornelia Sorabji, educated Somerville College, Oxford. Bachelor of Civil Law, Oxford. Called to the Bar, Lincoln's Inn, 1923. Died 1954.

2. Prime Minister Maharajah Chandra Shum Shere Jung Bahadur Rana, G.C.B., G.C.S.I., G.C.V.O., G.C.M.G., D.C.L. Oxford (1908), F.R.G.S. (1912). Honorary General in the British Army. In Nepal at this time the King was a nominal monarch, all power being in the hands of a hereditary Prime Minister.

3. In *A King's Story* by the Duke of Windsor (Cassell, 1951).

4. Edwin Landseer Lutyens, K.C.I.E., O.M., R.A., F.R.I.B.A. (1869–1944). Joint architect with Herbert Baker for the New Delhi government buildings, 1912. Work include the Whitehall Cenotaph, the British School of Art in Rome, Picture Gallery and South African War Memorial in Johannesburg, British Embassy in Washington. Principal architect to the Imperial War Graves Commission.

5. Herbert Baker, K.C.I.E., R.A., F.R.I.B.A. (1862–1946). Began his practice in South Africa. Joint architect with Sir Edwin Lutyens for the New Delhi government buildings. Later became architect to the Governments of South Africa, India and Kenya. Consultant, War Graves Commission.

6. Maharajah Sir Pertab Singh, G.C.S.I., G.C.V.O., K.C.B. (1845–1922). Great-uncle of the then Maharajah of Jodhpur. A.D.C. to Edward VII and George V. Honorary Major General in the British Army. From 1878 to 1902 Chief Minister of Marwar (Jodhpur). Served on staff, wounded and mentioned in despatches during Mohmand and Tirah campaigns. Created Maharajah of Idar, 1902. In 1911 he abdicated in order to become Regent during the minority of the Maharajah of Jodhpur. LL.D. Cambridge, D.C.L. Oxford.

7. Rao Rajah Hanut Singh, a world-famous polo player.

8. H. H. Maharaj Sri Ripudaman Singhji Malavendra of Nabha, F.R.G.S., M.R.A.S. Succeeded 1911. Member of the Viceroy's Legislative Council, 1906–1908. President of Indian National Social Conference, 1909. Deposed, 1924.

9. From the Nizam of Hyderabad: His Exalted Highness Asaf Jah Muzaffar-ul-Mulk Nizam-ul-Mulk Nizam-ud-Dowla Nawab Mir Sir Osman Ali Khan Fateh-Jung, G.C.S.I. (1886–1966). Succeeded 1911.

10. *Rufus Isaacs, 1st Marquess of Reading* by Montgomery Hyde (Heinemann, 1967), p. 369.

11. Jalal-ud-din Akbar (1542–1605). Third Emperor of the Timurid (Moghul) dynasty. Succeeded his father, Humayon, 1556. Consolidated the rule of his House. Founded the Dīn-Ilāhi, Universal Faith. Buried at Sikandra, near Agra.

CHAPTER IX

Pages 82–91

1. Henry Seymour Rawlinson, General Lord Rawlinson of Trent, G.C.B., G.C.V.O., K.C.M.G. (1864–1925), 1st Baron (created 1919), 2nd Baronet (created 1891). Commander-in-Chief, India, 1920–25.

2. John Marshall (1876–1958). Director General of Archaeology in India, 1902–31. Knighted, 1914.

3. Victor Alexander, 2nd Earl of Lytton, K.G., P.C., G.C.S.I., G.C.I.E. (1876–1947). Governor of Bengal, 1922–27.

4. A French doctor who taught a form of healing based on auto-suggestion. It became very fashionable.

5. James Scorgie Meston, K.C.S.I. (1865–1943). Lt. Governor of the United Provinces, 1912–18. Finance Member, Viceroy's Executive Council, 1918–19. Created Baron 1919.

6. James Lyle Mackay, 1st Earl of Inchcape, G.C.S.I., G.C.M.G., K.C.I.E. (1852–1932). In shipping from birth. Appointed to staff of Mackinnon Mackenzie, Calcutta, in 1874. President of Bengal Chamber of Commerce, 1890–93, then took charge of the London Office of the British India Company. In 1914 fused it with the Peninsular & Oriental Banking Corporation to form, with other companies, the P. & O. Steam Navigation Company. Viscount, 1924. Earl, 1929.

7. V. S. Srinivasa Sastri. Born 1869. A Madras Brahmin, head of The Servants Of India Society. Accompanied Mr. Montagu on his tour of India, 1918. Represented India at the Imperial Peace Conference, 1921. Privy Councillor, 1921. Toured the Dominions in 1922 to look into the rights of Indians. Agent for the Government of India in South Africa, 1926–29. Freeman of the City of London. Member of Round Table Conference, 1930–31.

8. *Rufus Isaacs, Marquess of Reading* by his son, Vol. II, p. 271.

9. His Highness Maharajah Dhiraj Bhupindra Singh, Maharajah of Patiala, G.C.S.I., G.C.I.E., G.C.V.O., G.B.E. (1891–1938). Served in Indian Expeditionary Force in World War I. Represented India at the League of Nations Assembly, 1925. Led Indian States Delegation to London Round Table Conference, 1930. Captained the M.C.C. at Bombay, 1926. Chancellor of the Chamber of Princes, 1926, 1930, 1933, 1935, 1937 till his death.

10. Muhi-ud-din Muhammed Aurangzeb Alamgir (1659–1707). Sixth Emperor of the Timurid (Moghul) dynasty. Succeeded 1659 after liquidating his brothers and imprisoning his father, Shah Jehan. Buried at Aurangabad in the Deccan.

11. Adjutant-General, Army Headquarters.

12. Air Vice-Marshall Sir John Maitland Salmond, K.C.B., C.M.G., C.V.O., D.S.O. Commanded R.A.F. in Iraq, 1922. Air Officer Commanding in Chief Air Defence of Great Britain, 1925–29. Chief of the Air Staff, 1930–33.

13. Dame Nellie Melba (1861–1931). Singer. Born Helen Porter Armstrong, near Melbourne, Australia. Pupil of Manuel Garcia and Madame Mathilde Marchesi, who launched her in Paris. First sang at Covent Garden (*Lucia di Lammermoor*), 1888. D.B.E. 1918. G.B.E. 1927. Raised £100,000 for the Red Cross in World War I.

CHAPTER X

Pages 92–98

1. His Highness Maharajah Dhirraju Tukoji Rae Holkar, G.C.I.E. Born 1891. Ruled over 9,500 square miles, population 850,000. Abdicated in favour of his son, 1926.

2. Sir Hukumchand.

3. John Perronet Thompson, M.A. Indian Civil Service. Political Secretary to the Government of India, 1922. Knighted, 1924.

4. His Highness Maharajadhiraja Sir Gulab Singh Bahadur, G.C.I.E., K.C.S.I. Born 1903. Succeeded as a minor, 1918.

5. Jawaharlal Nehru (1889–1964). Prime Minister of India and Minister for External Affairs, 1947–64. Educated Harrow School, Trinity College, Cambridge (M.A.). Barrister-at-Law, Inner Temple, 1912. Advocate, Allahabad High Court. Attended Bankipore Congress as delegate, beginning his political career, 1912. General Secretary, All India Congress Committee, 1923. Instrumental in committing Congress to goal of independence at Madras Congress, 1926. Founded Independence For India League, advocating complete severance of British connection, and was General Secretary, 1928. President, Lahore session of Congress when creed changed to complete independence,

12

1929. Sentenced to six months' imprisonment for part in Salt Laws Civil Disobedience, 1930; President, Lucknow session of Congress, 1936 and Faizpur session. Sentenced to four years imprisonment for Individual Satyagraha, 1940; released 1941. "Quit India" Resolution at A.I.C.C. Bombay session led to detention in Ahmednagar Fort, 1942–45. Elected Congress President for fourth time, 1946. Formed Interim Government and sworn in as Vice-President and Member in Charge, External Affairs, 2.9.1946. Became first Prime Minister of free India, August 15th, 1947. Bharat Ratna award, 1954. Elected to the Lok Sabha as Congress Party member for Phulpur constituency, U.P., 1957. Died May 27th, 1964.

6. *The Discovery of India* (Meridian Books Ltd., 1946).

CHAPTER XI

Pages 99–108

1. Pandit Moti Lal Nehru (1861–1931). A Kashmiri Brahmin and a distinguished lawyer. Supported the Indian National Congress from the first but took no active part in politics until the disturbances in the Punjaub in 1919. He then gave up his practice at the Bar and entered into the non-co-operation campaign. President of Congress, 1919. Chairman, All India Swaraj Party, 1925. Chairman of Nehru Report Committee, 1928. Imprisoned, 1930; released on grounds of ill-health.

2. Chitta Ranjan Das (1870–1925). A Hindu from Bengal, though not orthodox as he grew up in the Brahmo-Samaj movement. Called to the Bar but gave up his practice in 1919 to enter politics. President of Congress, 1922. Though of extreme left-wing views, he was never a communist and decided to join the Legislature in order to wreck from within. This induced the Bengal Government of 1924 to take over power from Ministers. Shortly before his death in 1925 he was endeavouring to negotiate a *modus vivendi* with the Bengal Government.

3. Arthur Hamilton Lee, 1st Viscount Lee of Fareham (cr. 1922), G.C.B., G.C.S.I. (1868–1947), Privy Councillor (1919). Originally in the Royal Artillery, followed by a distinguished career in diplomacy. Personal Secretary to Lloyd George, 1916. Director of Food Production, 1917. Member of the Imperial Cabinet. Chairman of several Royal Commissions in addition to the Commission on pay of public services in India. Trustee of the National Gallery and the Wallace Collection. Gave "Chequers" to the nation, 1921.

4. Much good work was done for widows by the Brahmo-Samaj and Prathana Samaj organisations in the nineteenth century and by The Servants Of India Society in the twentieth century.

5. Puggaree is the same as Pagii, – a turban – the former an anglicised spelling.

6. His Highness Air Vice-Marshall Shri Sir Umaid Singhji, G.C.S.I., G.C.I., K.C.V.O. (1911–1947). Chief of the Rhatores. Succeeded 1918. Full powers, 1923.

7. Carrying chairs borne by four men with poles over their shoulders.

8. Sir Syed Mahommed Hamid Ali, Khan, G.C.S.I., G.C.V.O., Nawab of Rampur (1875–1930). Succeeded at the age of ten. Knighted, 1908. Aide-de-camp to George V. Honorary Major General, 1929. Ruled over 892 square miles and population of 500,000.

9. His Highness Maharaja Sir Tashi Namgyal, K.C.I.E. Born 1893. Invested with ruling powers, 1918. In that year he married Kunzang Dechen, the daughter of a general in the Tibetan Army, grand-daughter of a Chief Minister of Tibet.

CHAPTER XII

Pages 109–117

1. Basil Philott Blackett, K.C.B. (1921). Finance Member, Viceroy's Executive Council, 1923–26. Representative in United States of His Majesty's Treasury, 1917–19. Officer of the Legion of Honour.

2. Lt.-Colonel C. Kennedy Crawford-Stuart, C.V.O., C.B.E., D.S.O. 10th Baluch Light Infantry. Military Secretary to Lord Reading, 1921–23.

3. Sir John Maffey, K.C.V.O., C.S.I., C.I.E. Chief Commissioner, North-West Frontier Province, 1921–24.

4. The Kaisar-i-Hind Medal was instituted by Queen Victoria in 1900 and bestowed for public service rendered in India without distinction of race or sex. There were two classes: (1) Gold, on the recommendation of the Secretary of State; and (2) Silver, on the recommendation of the Governor-General. An oval-shaped badge with the royal cypher of the sovereign and the words: "Kaisar-i-Hind for Public Services in India".

5. His Highness Sir Sawai Kishar Singh, K.C.S.I., Maharajah of Bharatpur (1899–1929. A Jat Ruler. Page to George V and Queen Mary at the Delhi Durbar, 1911. Knighted 1926. Ruled over 2,000 square miles and half-a-million people.

6. His Highness Thakur Sahib Sir Waghji Ravaji, G.C.I.E. Born 1858. Succeeded 1870. Ruled over 822 square miles and population of 90,000.

7. Baby Week Movement, inaugurated by Lady Reading in 1924, was the final outcome of maternity and baby welfare work started in a very small way by Miss Hewlett, a missionary in Amritsar in 1886. Very little was done to extend her work until 1918 when Miss Graham and Miss Griffin were given the task of training and supervising *Dais* (native midwives) in Delhi. Lady Chelmsford's appeal for funds launched in 1919 led to the first Maternity and Child Welfare Exhibition held in Delhi in 1920, when the Lady Chelmsford League for Maternity and Child Welfare was formed to share with the Red Cross Society the task of spreading education and propaganda in the provinces since the provincial governments did not feel they could spare money for these projects. Lady Reading greatly extended the movement and Baby Weeks, for which provincial Governors were made responsible, were held all over the country annually from 1924 onwards. These Weeks consisted of exhibitions in towns and large villages, at which propaganda posters, films and slides were shown and at which lecturers gave simple instruction in baby care. There were also baby shows with prizes. The training of midwives was not part of these exhibitions, though simple instruction was available to mothers for pre- and post-natal care. The Baby Week Movement was run by a Baby Week Council with headquarters at Delhi. In 1926 the Health School, started by Miss Graham and Miss Griffin in 1921, was moved to new premises, built from money collected by Lady Reading, and called the Lady Reading Health School. Here midwives were trained, and a model Welfare Centre was established to assist in the training of Health Visitors as well as midwives.

8. *The Men Who Ruled India, Vol. II, The Guardians* by Philip Woodruff (Jonathan Cape, 1954), p. 288.

9. The Most Reverend Foss Westcott, M.A., Lord Bishop of Calcutta and Metropolitan of India. His Bill was for the disestablishment of the Anglican Church in India.

10. Montagu Sherard Dawes Butler, K.C.S.I., C.V.O., C.I.E., C.B.E. (1873–1952). Indian Civil Service. President, Punjaub Legislative Council 1921–22. Secretary, Government of India, 1922–24. President, Council of State, 1924. Governor, Central Provinces and Berar, 1925–34. Governor of the Isle of Man, 1934–38. Master of Pembroke College, Cambridge, 1938–48.

11. Sir B. Narasimha Sarma. Born January 1867. Educated at Hindu College, Vizagapatam, Rajamundry College and Presidency College, Madras. Subsequently teacher, professor and at the Bar in Vizagapatam and Madras. Law Member of the Governor General's Executive Council, 1920–25. President, Railway Rates Advisory Committee, 1926.

CHAPTER XIII

Pages 118–127

1. Right Hon. Sir Shadi Lal (1874–1945). Privy Councillor, 1934. Knighted, 1921. Educated Balliol College, Oxford. Called to the Bar (Gray's Inn), 1899. Member of Punjaub Legislative Council, 1909 and 1912–13. Chief Justice, High Court of Judicature, Lahore, 1920–34. Honorary Bencher of Gray's Inn, 1935.

2. Ranjit Singh (1780–1839). He founded a Sikh kingdom north of the Indus and conquered Kashmir. This kingdom was lost by his descendants to the British.

3. Henry Montgomery Lawrence (1806–57). Elder brother of John Lawrence (q.v.). Commanded the Sikh contingent at the Kabul disaster in 1840. Resident at the Court of Nepal, 1843. Fought in the 1st and 2nd Sikh Wars. Agent to the Governor-General in Rajputana, 1850. Chief Commissioner, Oudh, 1857. Killed during the siege of the Residency, Lucknow, Indian Sepoy Mutiny.

4. His Highness Maharana Adhiraja Sir Fateh Singhji, G.C.S.I. (1849–1930). Succeeded 1885. Ruled over 12,691 square miles and over one million population.

5. *Annals and Antiquities of Rajasth'an* by Colonel James Tod (1823).

6. Aboriginal tribes living in the hills and jungles of Central India. An ancient non-Aryan people, once known as Nishadas. Animist by religion, they are now being gradually Hinduised.

7. His Highness Sir Govind Singh of Datia, K.C.S.I. Born 1886. Title of Maharajah recognised as hereditary, 1865. He succeeded in 1907. Gave an annual contribution of Rs. 25,000 to the British forces in World War I. Ruler over 912 square miles with population of 170,000.

8. Hyder Ali (1722–82). A Muslim adventurer, son of an officer of the Mysore Hindu government. In 1755 became head of the Army, extended his power till at the death of the Rajah in 1766 he gained supremacy in fact, if not in name. From 1769 to 1784 he and his son Tipu fought against the British. After Hyder's death, Tipu carried on till the Treaty of Mangalore, 1784. War began again in 1786 and ended in the Treaty of Seringapatam, 1792. A final and rapid war (concluded in two months) put an end to Tipu Sultan who was slain in battle and the State of Mysore returned to the Hindu ruling family whom Hyder had displaced to begin with.

9. His Highness Sir Krishnaraja Wadyar, G.C.S.I., G.B.E. Born 1884. Chancellor, Benares University and Mysore University since 1895. Ruled over 29,444 square miles and population of six million.

10. Freeman Freeman-Thomas, 1st Marquess of Willingdon, P.C., G.C.S.I., G.C.M.G., G.C.I.E. (1866–1941). Governor of Bombay, 1913; of Madras, 1919–24. Governor-General of Canada, 1926–31. Viceroy of India, 1931–36. Lord Warden of the Cinque Ports, 1936–41.

11. Robert Clive (1725–74). Went to India in 1743 as a clerk in the service of the East India Company. Rose to be Governor of Bengal and to consolidate British power in India. A military commander as well as an administrator. Accused of bribery, but cleared. Raised to an Irish Peerage as Baron Clive of Plassey, 1762. Died by his own hand in great depression as a result of indulgence in opium.

12. These nuns were Portuguese and their convent remained a tiny outpost of Portuguese India. St. Thomas the Apostle is supposed to have been martyred by Brahmins on St. Thomas' Mount.

CHAPTER XIV

Pages 128–136

1. The annexation of Burma took place over a period of sixty years: Arakan and Tenasserim, 1826; Pegu, 1852; Upper Burma (Kingdom of Thebaw), 1886. Independence of Burma, 1947.
2. Megan Lloyd George, J.P., LL.D., M.P., younger daughter of David Lloyd George, 1st Earl Lloyd George. She represented Anglesey in the House of Lords as a Liberal from 1929–31, as an Independent Liberal from 1931–45, as Labour from 1945–51. She represented Camarthen in the Labour interest from 1957 till her death in 1966.
3. Rabindranath Tagore. Author, poet and musician. Born 1861. Knighted 1915. Founded Santi Niketan, a centre for the development of the arts in India, which became an international institute for the study of sociology as well. Nobel Prize for literature, 1913. Ardent worker for Indian independence.
4. Mahommed Ali Jinnah (1876–1948). *Qaid-i-Azam.* Called to the Bar, Lincoln's Inn, 1896. Member of the Imperial Legislative Council from 1910. President, All India Muslim League, 1920 and from 1934. Attended the Round Table Conference, 1929–30. Member of the Legislative Assembly and Leader of the Muslim League Party until August, 1947. Founder of Pakistan and first Governor-General, 1947–48.
5. His Highness Maharaj Rana Udai Bhan Singh Lokindra. Born 1893. Succeeded 1911. K.C.S.I. (1918). A Jat Ruler. State, 1,200 square miles; population, 230,188.
6. *Pagri:* a turban. A Sikh in full dress wears his beard brushed round the chin and held in position by a net. The Punjaubi *pagri* carries a pleated fan of starched material at one side.
7. William Hesketh Lever, 1st Viscount Leverhulme (1851–1947). Chairman of Lever Bros. and founder of Port Sunlight. Baronet, 1911. Baron, 1917. Viscount, 1922.
8. Horatio Norman Bolton, C.S.I., C.I.E. Chief Commissioner, North-West Frontier Province.
9. Lt.-Colonel Francis Henry Humphreys, G.C.V.O., K.C.M.G., K.B.E. Born 1879. Political Agent, Khyber, 1919. H.B.M.'s first Envoy Extraordinary and Minister Plenipotentiary at the Court of Afghanistan. Later High Commissioner and Commander-in-Chief, Iraq.

CHAPTER XV

Pages 137–145

1. Lt.-Colonel (later Sir Thomas) Carey-Evans, M.C. Indian Medical Service. Married Olwen, eldest daughter of 1st Earl Lloyd George. Surgeon to H.E. Lord Reading, 1921–24.
2. Geoffrey Harvey de Montmorency, K.C.V.O., C.I.E., C.B.E. Indian Civil Service. Private Secretary to H.E. Lord Reading, 1923–25. Later Governor of the Punjaub.
3. Lt.-Colonel W. W. Muir, M.V.O., O.B.E. 15th Sikhs. Comptroller to the Household to H.E. Lord Reading, 1921–26.
4. Colonel R. B. Worgan, C.S.I., C.V.O., D.S.O. Military Secretary to H.E. Lord Reading, 1923–26.
5. The Chinese suite from *Casse Noisette*, Tchaikovsky.

6. Atul Chandra Chatterjee, Indian Civil Service. Born 1874. C.I.E. Knighted, 1925. Member of Viceroy's Executive Council, 1923–25. High Commissioner for India in London, 1925.

CHAPTER XVI

Pages 146–155

1. Sir Hari Singh. Born 1895. In 1924 he was the heir apparent to the Gadi of Kashmir, succeeding his uncle in 1925 as His Highness the Shree Maharajah Hari Singh Bahadur, K.C.I.E., K.C.V.O.
2. Yvonne FitzRoy's Diary.
3. Frederick Edwin Smith, 1st Earl of Birkenhead (created 1922), G.C.S.I. Privy Councillor. Solicitor General, 1915. Attorney General, 1915–16 and again in 1919. Lord High Chancellor, 1919–23. Secretary of State for India, 1924–28. Baronet, 1918. Baron, 1918. Viscount, 1921.
4. Yvonne FitzRoy's Diary.
5. *Annals and Antiquities of Rajasth'an* by Colonel James Tod (1823).
6. George Nathaniel Curzon (1859–1925). Under-Secretary of State for India, 1891–92. Under-Secretary of State for Foreign Affairs, 1895–98. Baron, 1898. Viceroy of India, 1899–1905. Viscount, 1911. Secretary of State for Foreign Affairs, 1919–24. Marquess, 1921.
7. Small two-wheeled pony-cart.

CHAPTER XVII

Pages 156–163

1. Major-General His Royal Highness Prince Arthur Frederick Albert of Connaught, K.G., P.C., G.C.M.G., G.C.V.O. (1883–1938). Only son of H.R.H. the Duke of Connaught. He married H.R.H. Princess Alexandria Victoria (1891–1959), eldest daughter of the Duke of Fife and Princess Louise, Princess Royal, eldest daughter of Edward VII. Governor-General of South Africa, 1920–24.
2. Sir David Yule (1838–1928). 1st Baronet, created 1922. Member of Andrew Yule and Co., Calcutta.
3. Sir Harry MacLennan Lauder (1870–1950). Singer. Started as a mill boy in a flax-spinning mill at Arbroath, then worked as a miner. Started singing at local concerts. Became renowned in Scotland and later in England. Composed words and music of all his songs. Knighted, 1919.
4. Sir Ellice Victor Sassoon. 3rd Baronet (cr. 1909). Succeeded his father, 1924. Educated Harrow and Trinity College, Cambridge. Chairman, E. D. Sassoon & Co. Captain, R.A.F., in World War I. Member of the Legislative Assembly, India, 1922–23, and in 1926–29. Member of the Royal Commission for investigation of labour conditions in India, 1929. Race-horse owner and breeder. Winner of the Derby.
5. Maharani of Cooch-Behar. Indira, daughter of H.H. Sayaji Rao III. Gaekwar of Baroda (see Chapter V. Note 20). Widow of Maharajah Bhup Bahadur Sir Jitendra Maharajah of Cooch Behar. He died December 20th, 1922. She died 1967.
6. Lt.-Commander Sir Henry Warden Stanley Chilcote. Knighted 1922. Member of Parliament, Walton Division, Liverpool, from 1918.
7. Robert Horne (1871–1940). Later Viscount Horne of Slamannan (1937). Lawyer and politician. Minister of Labour in Lloyd George's government. President of the Board of Trade, 1920. Chancellor of the Exchequer, 1921.

8. Oswald Ernald Mosley, 6th Baronet (cr. 1781). Succeeded 1928. Member of Parliament (Conservative), 1918–22. Independent, 1922–24. Labour, 1924–31. After which he founded the Black Shirt movement, the British form of Fascism. He married (first) Cynthia, second daughter of Marquess Curzon of Kedleston.

9. Walter John Montagu-Douglas-Scott, later 8th Duke of Buccleuch, 10th of Queens-bury, K.T., P.C., G.C.V.O. Born 1894. Married Vreda Esther, elder daughter of the late Major William Lascelles, Scots Guards.

10. George Joachim Goschen, 2nd Viscount, G.C.S.I., G.C.I.E., C.B.E. (1866–1952). Governor of Madras, 1924–29.

11. Captain R. C. Burton, Coldstream Guards. He was Aide-de-Camp to Lord Reading for the full term of H.E.'s office. He was responsible for the decorations and design of the "Feast of Lanterns" in 1924.

12. Ivor Miles Windsor Clive, 2nd Earl of Plymouth. Married Lady Irene Charteris, 3rd daughter of the 11th Earl of Wemyss. The mother-in-law accompanying the Plymouths to India was Mary Constance, daughter of the Hon. Percy Scawen Wyndham, M.P.

13. William Riddell Birdwood, Indian Army, G.C.B., G.C.S.I., G.C.M.G., G.C.V.O., D.S.O., C.I.E. (1865–1951). Commanded the Australian and New Zealand Army Corps, 1914–18. General, 1917. Commanded Dardanelles Army, 1915–16. Baronet, 1919. Field Marshal, 1925. Commander-in-Chief, India, 1925–30. Master of Peter-house College, Cambridge, 1931–38. Baron, 1938.

CHAPTER XVIII

Pages 164–169

1. Frederick Alexander Whyte. Born 1883. President, Legislative Assembly, India, 1920–25. Member of Parliament for Perth City, 1910–18. Knighted, 1922.

2. Vithalbhai Jhaverbhai Patel (1873–1933). First elected President, Indian Legislative Assembly. Educated Ahmedabad and England. Member of Bombay Corporation. Chairman, Schools Committee, 1923–24. Bombay Legislative Council and Imperial Council. President of Bombay Corporation, 1924–25. Chairman, Reception Committee, Special Bombay Congress, 1918. Member, Civil Disobedience Committee which toured India, 1922. Elected President, Legislative Assembly, August, 1925. Re-elected President, Legislative Assembly, January, 1927.

Index

(References to Notes in brackets)